The
Parables
of
Harris

The
Parables
of
Harris

Peter and Fiona Horrobin
&
Harris!

Lancaster Editorials Ltd

This book is published by:
Lancaster Editorials Ltd
P.O.Box 761,
Preston
PR3 0WX
England

1 2 3 4 5 6 7 8 9

ISBN 0-9546380-0-X

Printed in England by Clays Ltd., St. Ives Plc.

Contents

Preface

The day Harris came home our lives were changed for ever! From the moment he put his first huge paw over our thresh-hold, and took control of the home, we knew we were in for an adventure. And what an adventure it has proved to be!

Laughter and labradors are never far apart! Harris has been an endless source of fun and entertainment. Like most dogs, he's far from being perfect, but we have learned some wonderful lessons through his antics and efforts. And in spite of his naughtiness, we have found him to be utterly lovable. He doesn't need words to be able to talk!

From his earliest days we began to turn these lessons into living parables. As we used them to illustrate the teaching we both give, in various parts of the world, people easily absorbed and understood important truths as they have laughed with us at our experiences. We began to realise that when Harris became part of the family he also became part of the work we are involved in.

This last summer the family were helpless with laughter at seeing me being dragged along the beach by an enthusiastic Harris at the end of his lead. Suddenly he ran through some shallow water and across a patch of quick-sands!

Harris scampered easily across the surface of the sand - his weight spread evenly across four legs - but my 200lbs on only two legs was more than the sand could take! I sank quickly up to my hips, threw myself fully clothed flat across the beach to avoid sinking any further in the sand and, having recovered from the initial shock, allowed Harris to drag me out of the sand by the lead! I could hardly breathe because I was laughing so much. I was utterly convulsed with the humour of the situation! If only it had been on video!!

No-one would expect that such an undignified experience could be almost the highlight of the holiday, but Harris has a knack of transforming the most innocent of situations into a memorable moment! Harris has certainly taught us to laugh at ourselves.

This book contains some of those memorable moments - and some of the lessons we have learned from the experience. We trust you will enjoy reading it as much as we have enjoyed living it!

Peter and Fiona Horrobin   *October 2003*

Chapter 1
Harris Comes Home
Fiona's Story

I woke up in the middle of the night feeling restless. Half awake, half asleep, I became acutely aware of my husband's pale and lined face. Inside me, I voiced a deep desire to try and do something which would help relieve the pressure of his relentless hours of work and problem solving.

It seemed that in Peter's position, as the head of a large charity, he had to take the worst end of all the organisational problems and as the saying goes, the buck always stopped with him! He was exhausted.

I had hardly voiced my heartfelt plea when into my mind, very clearly, came the words "a black lab!" Outside of work, the loves of Peter's life are fishing, football, classic cars and black labs! It was years since he had owned such a dog. Our lives of travel and endless meetings had put an end to any possibility of being a dog owner again.

I laughed in my sleep! A black lab! What a joke! At best, it was a good dream that would be forgotten by morning!

My husband, Peter, is a visionary character with an ability to create and make things happen all around him. Hence his life is mostly one long whirlwind of activity. Since starting to work full time for a Christian Charity, which was set up to help people, he has spent countless hundreds of hours, giving of himself on behalf of others.

Many who came for help had been emotionally, sexually, mentally or physically abused or had suffered some extreme trauma in their life. We longed to bring comfort, healing and restoration to these hurting people.

Our belief in a personal and loving God, who is not remote, distant or ignorant of the pain people suffer, led us on a life-time journey of developing places of safety for those in need, training teams of people with caring hearts and establishing programmes which would teach, train and equip others to do this work also. To see battered lives restored and fulfilled in their potential, made this life-work magnificently rewarding.

But as with anything worthwhile, as it grows in size and effectiveness, so also do the consequential demands and, occasionally, the problems! Being a leader with a multitude of responsibilities is a long way from being a bed of roses, and the day-to-day pressures can be huge!

It was not only the demands of people that were overtaking us, we were also being swamped by technology! We eventually capitulated to every technical aid available and in addition to the daily mail-bag, the telephone, answering machines, fax machines, mobile phones, text messages and endless e-mails were beginning to control our lives - all of course were supposed to be "absolutely essential"! But as the years went by we hadn't fully appreciated what a draining effect all these pressures were having on us.

Modern technology demanded instant responses and direct personal e-mails produced a limitless need for hours of written correspondence. Gone was the secretarial buffer! As Peter's wife, I saw first hand the effect of all the many frustrations and pressures caused by continuous hard work, long-haul jet travel, endless commitment to others and often the pain of being misunderstood or misrepresented.

The reward of seeing so many lives touched, blessed and healed, however, was reward enough, but in the middle of it all, the God we served knew that we had human needs too. And He was about to provide for some of them in a rather unusual way!

I don't usually remember dreams. But the morning after this half-awake-half-asleep dream, the picture of the black lab persisted in my mind. I couldn't shake it off as I went to work and instead of going away, it was developing from a dream into a well thought out vision and finally a plan!

Peter's birthday was coming up soon, we had no more long-distance travel plans for a while. I convinced myself that if there was ever going to be a time for such a crazy adventure this was an ideal moment to buy a puppy!

My thoughts raced on. At home we had a lovely big farmhouse kitchen with a warm stove which never went out, a massive garden with a paddock attached and there was always someone in our house when we travelled. If they liked dogs and would be willing to look after a four-legged member of the family while we were away, then maybe this joke was not so silly after all!

I stupidly ventured to share my thoughts with the two friends I was working with that day. To my amazement, rather than laugh and scold me for even thinking about such a crazy thing, they leapt at the idea. I immediately backtracked saying, "well it's just a joke. With our lifestyle, we couldn't possibly. It's a nice thought, but it's out of the question really. Peter wouldn't agree. He's far too busy and even if he did agree I wouldn't know where to find a black lab puppy anyway!"

As far as I was concerned that was it. I had successfully dismissed this whole dog idea with a few minutes of sensible rational thinking. But, I had reckoned without my two friends. They thought it was a brilliant idea and in a flash one of them had opened the yellow business pages of the local telephone directory and responded to the advertisement of a black labrador breeder. And, yes, they did have some pups right now which will be old enough to leave their mother in about a week's time!

She joyfully announced the news and said that we could go and see them right now and choose one! And, what was more, she had already made an appointment! Help! Things were moving far too fast for me. Only a few hours ago it was just a dream - now we were headed for an appointment at the breeding kennels.

What was I doing? I needed to get on with the job in hand for the day and forget this dog business. There was far too much to do. I began to take some security in the thought that nothing's going to happen anyway because Peter would NEVER agree!

My friend went up to speak with Peter in his office. Totally contrary to expectation and to my utter amazement, he agreed to go with us on "a very important trip", without being told in advance what it was for!

My husband's character was such that he would normally resist being taken unawares or having to respond to sudden unplanned interruptions! His feet were securely on the ground. Before agreeing to anything he would want to know that his precious time was being used for sensible reasons. As he came down the stairs to the waiting car, he looked at me for confirmation that my friend's request was genuine and important. I found myself nodding furiously.

But inside there was a growing sense of panic! "God, was it really you that gave me this idea?" I wanted to believe that I had got it all wrong. But somehow or other I couldn't bring myself to agree with my own concerns!

We drove for nearly an hour and it was clear Peter had no idea whatsoever where he was going, let alone what the trip was all about. My friends were so excited. They were doing their best to control occasional bouts of laughter, but inside me was a growing sense of self-doubt and panic - life was about to change!

When we were close to the breeding kennels, my friend suddenly produced a blanket and put it over Peter's head. He didn't know how to react and was clearly a little frustrated at having spent so much time away from the office just to be the participant in some form of practical joke! It took me several minutes to convince him that this was to be a good experience and that it would be a surprise he will enjoy.

As we led him down the garden path of the breeding kennels, with the blanket still covering his head, the sound of yapping could be clearly heard. The pups had given the game away. Moments later a bright faced lady met us at the gate and cheerily said, "well here they are".

The blanket was removed and Peter's face looked a picture of utter disbelief as he gazed at the tiny black puppies poking their heads over a wooden partition, all with their tails wagging and all eager to meet him. He looked at me and them in disbelief! I could read some of his thoughts "Are you serious? Do you mean it? What's this all about? We couldn't possibly . . . . .?"

The lady cut across his unspoken words and asked, "Which one would you like?" There were black and chocolate labradors in the litter, but the chocolate ones were already spoken for and not for sale. The choice was between three black ones. I picked one out which I thought had a pretty face and seemed to have a bit of determination to be noticed!

He snuggled into Peter's arms and the bond was immediate. We picked up the others in turn, but the first one had our hearts. Looking back at that first encounter, he was a fearless little puppy and quite a rascal too, but I had no experience of picking puppies and Peter was still shell shocked!

The puppy was just over eight weeks old but we couldn't take him till he was nine weeks old on the following Saturday. And just at that moment, we needed to recover from the shock of the decision that we seemed to have just made. We needed to do some hard thinking and make sure we were not just acting out of impulse or stupidity. We needed to count the cost of giving this trusting little dog a decent life.

At the same time as pacing around the kennels, attempting to come to terms with the consequences of this sudden intrusion into our lives, we could not hide our joy and excitement at the possibility of once again having a dog in the family. But in reality this little puppy had already entered our hearts, he was ours. It would only be a matter of time before he was at home by the fire!

How would we know which puppy was which, when we came to collect him? We were already keen to make sure that that we would get the same puppy as the one we had chosen today? We didn't want any other puppy! "Don't worry", the lady cheerily said as she daubed his forehead with a bright blob of fluorescent pink nail varnish, "this will mark him out as yours!"

We went home in a flurry of excitement and panic! We could hardly believe it when all our various friends, team members and family, without exception, applauded the decision. Perhaps, in retrospect, some were kindly remaining quiet, saving their judgement till later, after Peter and Fiona had come to their senses!

However, Peter and I were happily in our element, our minds full of what we would need in order to bring up a black lab! So, it was that we went down to the local pet shop and bookshop to buy everything we could get hold of on how to bring up the most perfectly trained black labrador ever!

Time stood still during the following week. Looking forward to Saturday was like looking forward to something exciting when we were children and thinking the day would never come! But come it did and bright and early we were off to the kennels to collect our pup.

His name was going to be 'Harris'! There he was waiting for us with his dash of pink nail varnish on his head. Yes, this was our pup, no mistaking. We like to think his enthusiasm to see us was because he recognised us, but he probably reacted to every visitor with the same excitement!

Following final instructions from the kennel owner, we picked up our little bundle of fur in his new doggy blanket and told him of the wonderful life that lay ahead of him with us, his new owners! He was perfectly behaved on the journey home and has always been a good traveller in the car ever since.

Once home, he immediately wanted to play. I watched Peter, totally absorbed with this little puppy, who innocently demanded we gave him time and attention, despite everything else that was going on in our lives.

I sighed with relief. "God, that really was you who gave me the idea. This little puppy is the only thing I know of that can divert Peter's attention from the problems and pressures of work and bring him joy and fun at the same time".

I reflected on how good God is. In the midst of our toil, He wants us to have good things and He brought the perfect antidote into our lives to counteract the busyness, the problems and the hours of sitting at computers and coping with the artefacts of technology which are now so much a part of the age we live in.

Little did we know it then, but we were about to embark on a wonderful journey with our dog Harris, a journey on which we would learn more about ourselves, more about God and more about living life to the full than we could ever have done without him.

Harris truly made his home with us. I think he must have decided he would look after us and he has been and is the source of much joy and, however, occasional trouble as well! Three years on, we could not imagine life without him.

They say, do not have a labrador if you do not want to laugh. How true that is! Harris has kept our life full of entertainment, colour and fun. God is so good, He knew exactly what we needed - a four legged friend who has the capacity to make all problems look small and to bring a smile to our faces, even in the midst of the worst of difficulties. We hope as we share the adventures of Harris, you too will enjoy the laughter and lessons one little (now very big) dog can bring!

The book has been written between us and is full of tales and adventures which have kept us laughing as we have set out to have the very best trained lab, but have ended up being the very best trained owners, courtesy of our very characterful black lab, Harris.

Chapter 2
Harris Comes Home
Peter's Version

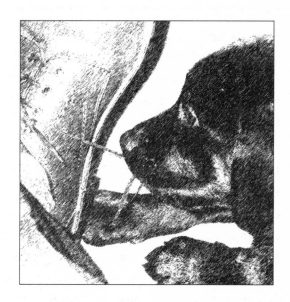

The 21st September 2000 was an ordinary sort of day.
Or so I thought! No meetings, just a day in the office
dealing with correspondence and getting ready for the
next event in my diary. Completely unknown to me,
however, a black labrador was giving birth - a very
normal event at the Crowlands Labradors maternity unit
- five black puppies, two chocolate and two golden. But,
unknown to me at the time, one of those black puppies
was destined to turn my life upside down!

Fiona (Fi) and I have always loved dogs and remember with much affection dogs from earlier days - Labradors for me that rejoiced in the names of Sam, Noah and Job and for Fi a Cairn called Tweedie and an English Setter called Jasper that came from an impeccable Anglican background, having spent its early weeks of life in the vicarage.

Often we had talked of having another dog, but had always concluded that it would be unfair to introduce a dog to our current lifestyle - with all the meetings, extensive travel and much time having to be spent away from home.

We were just a little jealous of friends who had managed to combine a job that entailed lots of travelling with handling a wonderful black labrador, who one day called at the door of their farmhouse as a stray, realised what a good home he had found and took up residence for the rest of his life.

Unknown to me, Fi had been taking a long hard look at the pressures on our life, our increasing years and lack of healthy exercise - not to mention our steadily increasing waistlines! She had obviously been wondering what to give me for my birthday - when out of the blue she had had the idea that a puppy in the family could help with both the exercise and the waistlines as well as initiate a much needed change of lifestyle!

She was seriously concerned, however, that having a dog might interfere with our work, but then if God was in the idea, surely He could take care of the ministry as well? Of course, I was completely oblivious at that stage to the plot that was being hatched behind my back and was steaming ahead with planning the programme for the following year without making any allowances for a black labrador in the family!

My birthday was only five days away - though this fact had hardly registered in my consciousness as I sat at my desk. I've reached the age when most birthdays are just another date on the diary - a sort of reminder that the years are passing without being of great significance. There were much more important things to do than think about birthdays!

I was just beginning to get down to an afternoon's paper work when, suddenly, there was a knock on the office door. One of the staff burst in with an urgent message from Fi. Something important had come up. Could I go immediately - it might take a couple of hours? I had a quick consultation with my secretary, changed the plans for the afternoon and, to my own amazement, said, "Yes!" I had no idea where I was going.

Outside a car was waiting. I was driven about thirty miles, and when we were close to an unknown destination a blanket was put over my head! I was then led by the hand, unable to see where I was going, feeling like a cross between a fool and a criminal.

When the blanket was removed I was standing in front

of a pen full of adorable black labrador puppies! From that moment on heart ruled the head, the battle was over and all that remained was to select one of them!

There was a full litter of puppies to choose from - which one was it going to be? We did pray, but even with the help of prayer, assessing the potential character of a labrador puppy seemed an impossible task. One almost felt guilty for rejecting any of them - they were all adorable.

If I was going to have a pup at all, I wanted it to be male, and one of the dogs in the litter did seem to have just a little bit more spunk and intelligence than the others. After much deliberation the decision was made - a blob of pink identifying nail varnish was dabbed on his head to distinguish him from the others, a cheque changed hands and no longer was this bundle of fur just one of the litter - this one was going to be ours! He would be old enough to collect on Saturday.

When the cold light of the following day dawned, however, I began to have lots of second thoughts. A look at the diary for the following year confirmed what a crazy decision we had made. Both of us are away from home so often. It would be cruel to put a puppy in kennels every time we went off on our travels. These and many other potential problems surfaced thick and fast, but one by one they were overcome - especially with the promise of help from a house and puppy sitter for the times when we were going to be away. The pup was coming to stay!

Now for a name. We tried all the obvious doggy names, but none seemed to fit our pup's character. We wanted something distinguished and different, but something which also meant something to us personally.

Almost simultaneously Fi and I thought about our annual holidays in Scotland on the Isle of Harris. Suddenly it seemed as though the name had chosen itself. Harris, of course, it was obvious. Our puppy was no longer an un-named bundle of fur and sharp puppy teeth - he was going to be called Harris!

He stayed with his Mum for another five days and then, on my birthday, we went to collect him. Leaving the rest of the litter behind and travelling in the car on the journey home was no problem for our Harris. He quickly settled into his new home - perhaps he did miss his Mum a little and maybe he missed his other puppy-mates a bit more, but he hardly seemed to notice. Independence could have been his second name.

From day one he made himself at home, fed well and slept all night in the kitchen in front of our warm Raeburn oil-fired cooker. He was already master of the house and made himself thoroughly at home.

Having made the decision to get Harris, we determined that we would take on the task of bringing him up seriously. A flurry of training manuals on how to bring up Labradors mounted up on the kitchen table. They gave us oodles of information and lots of advice, much of which was conflicting!

Nevertheless, we must have got some things right, for house training came easily. Harris seemed determined to please, was ever curious and was always ready for a game - at least until he collapsed, temporarily exhausted, into a black velvet heap of puppy-sleep.

We quickly found out that Harris really did have that extra bit of spunk I had been looking for - he was definitely not going to be a couch potato! Many is the time since then that we have thought a little less spunk would have been helpful - but then he wouldn't have been Harris, would he?

Chapter 3
Harris Takes Over!

Many a day, we sat at our farmhouse kitchen table looking at Harris on his rug and warming himself by the fire. In spite of the responsibility of extra daily routines and walks, we often expressed how glad we were he had come into our lives.

He made himself instantly 'at home' as though he knew right from the beginning that this was the home where he belonged, that these people looking after him were his rightful owners and that if these are his rightful owners then he has every right to the best chair in the house as well!

Achieving the comfort of the best chair became one of his primary targets in life and having achieved his objective he would snuggle into it as if it had been put there just for him!

He really did make himself perfectly at home. He would look at us through those huge, brown, doleful eyes of his, in total disbelief that we would do such a cruel thing, when we lifted him off the chair and gently ushered him back onto the floor! But then he would try to divert our attention and when he thought we weren't looking would find his way back to that place of special comfort. But if by then we were busy in a different part of the house, even the special comfort of his favourite chair was of no interest to him, for where we were is where he wanted to be. Harris's real comfort and security was in being with his owners.

If we were going out in the car, he loved to sit in the front seat, preferably with one paw over the driver's arm. Harris exuded an "I'm in charge" attitude and he never let anything or anyone go unnoticed. In fact, he so much wanted to be in charge that his desire to come to the front of the car was becoming a problem. He could be quite distracting to the driver and, potentially therefore, quite dangerous.

I knew when Harris arrived that we would have to put aside a small amount of extra money to pay for his food and various other doggy expenditures. That was part of the cost of having a dog. But Peter had not budgeted, however, on having to buy a new car!

He's driven Volvos for years. He quickly realised that our ageing saloon was not up to the task, so he began to look around for a Volvo estate. When he saw the prices of new cars he had to look the other way fast. So he began to study the advertisements and ring round all the local dealers with details of what we were looking for. None were very hopeful of finding a good car within our price range. The salesmen always seemed to lapse into a rather embarrassed silence when they were told how little we wanted to pay!

We wanted a low-mileage estate car - the sort you can put a dog-gate in, so we could keep Harris safely in a confined area at the back, away from the driving seat. Peter didn't hold out much hope of finding what we wanted. But surprisingly, before very long, a local Volvo agent rang with details of a much older example of the model we wanted, that they were having to take in part-exchange for a new car.

He seemed slightly embarrassed at the idea of putting such an old car in his show-room, so he offered it to us at a very good price if we were able to take it straight away. The price was just right. The car had a very low mileage and was ideal for the job.

With a new dog-gate fitted Harris quickly became accustomed to going out in what was clearly "his" car! The car was his perfect second home and we only had to walk towards the door for him to shoot up, cock his head on one side, giving us one of those amazingly characterful looks with his almond eyes, which said

"Am I coming too?" As soon as the tailgate was lifted he would be in like a flash, reserving his place for the journey.

We had learned from the breeders that Harris was from a long line of working dogs. So it was no surprise, therefore, that he seemed permanently on the alert, keeping us under constant vigil, always ready for whatever was happening next. If we sat at the table to eat our meal, he would come and lay at full stretch underneath it, keeping us reminded of the fact that he was part of us and went where we went.

When we went to bed, he recognised the routine of the kettle going on for the late-night drink, the tidying up of the lounge, the turning off of the TV and preparing for the nightly shut-down. As we busied ourselves with the routines he would go into a doleful mood and make us feel guilty for leaving him behind! How could his doggy eyes speak so clearly? But they did!

Harris very quickly knew us through and through. He understood all our movements and very accurately read our minds about what we were going to do next. He also knew how he could persuade us to give him the last little bit of a favourite meal or snack. He just had to give us one of those irresistible looks, with his head cocked on one side, and he had our attention.

Ice cream has proved to be one of his favourite recreational snacks and Peter's love for his dog has meant that on many occasions three ice creams now have to be bought instead of two. Against all the training rules, it seemed to us that sharing things like this with him was part of the joy of having a dog.

The remains of the Sunday roast have always been his very favourite sharing opportunity! Harris drools when Peter picks at the bones of the chicken or a joint of lamb and says to Harris "some for you and some for me". Then a very, very contented dog finds his way to a warm patch of sunshine or to his master's feet, passing the time contentedly, while Peter reads the newspaper or watches the news.

Harris had struck oil when he came to live with us! He had it made. The day that the pink nail varnish went on his head meant a life of labrador luxury and fun. Belonging to Peter would mean life would never be dull, never be boring and these two adventuresome spirits would challenge each other endlessly, bringing colour and adventure to life.

Back in the farmhouse kitchen, absorbing just how Harris had made himself entirely at home with us, we mulled over one very wonderful truth about our life as Christians. Just as we chose Harris, that momentous day back in November 2000, and the pink nail varnish singled him out as belonging to us, so our God sought after us individually to put the stamp of His ownership upon us.

And just as we were excited and overjoyed at owning Harris and developing a relationship with him, so our

God is overjoyed at owning us and having a relationship with us. Just as we anticipated the potential and fun there would be with Harris alongside us sharing the activities of life, so our God anticipated the plans, purposes and partnership there would be for Him to enjoy with us.

As we have spent hundreds of hours walking and adventuring with Harris, we have often reminded ourselves of the pink nail varnish day and how grateful we are to our God for that stamp of his ownership there is on our lives and the joy we have in the biggest and most exciting of life's adventures - partnering together with Him.

Chapter 4
Harris's First Parable

Harris quickly found his way into our hearts. He was, of course, the best puppy in all the world - in spite of doing all the naughty things that puppies always do. But one day I became aware that God might have had a hidden agenda in allowing us the privilege of extending the family circle to include Harris, at the same time as continuing with a job which meant us having to be away from home on so many occasions.

One day, shortly after his arrival, I was typing away in my office at home. Fi was out at work and I had left

Harris asleep in the kitchen. Something prompted me that Harris might still be rather lonely after so recently leaving behind his brothers and sisters, so I picked up my lap-top computer and went to work in the kitchen with him.

Harris didn't stir when I entered the kitchen. He was enjoying the oblivion of deep puppy sleep, stretched out full-length with his back soaking up the warm comfort of his substitute mother - the Raeburn cooker!

I sat down at the kitchen table and carried on typing on my computer. I was quickly absorbed again in an important piece of writing. But after a while I became aware that something had changed. I was so absorbed in what I was doing that I struggled for a moment to think what it was.

Then I realised my feet were getting warm! I looked down to see that Harris had silently got up from his place of warmth and comfort by the Raeburn and was now lying across my toes under the chair. All his warmth was being transferred to my feet! I smiled with deep affection as I stretched my hand down, stroked his head and tickled him behind the ears. He was obviously pleased that I had come down and joined him in the kitchen.

It was then that it happened. I was suddenly aware that God was speaking to me - right into my spirit. His voice was clear and unmistakeable. "Harris has left his comfort zone to come and sit at your feet. Are you

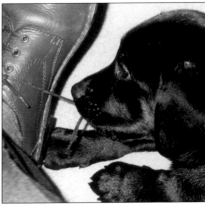

Fun &
Games

*Harris
meets
Mr. Jinks*

*Harri
enjoy
th
cand*

willing to leave your comfort zone to come and sit at My feet?"

My typing was suddenly no longer important. For a time the significance of Harris lying at his master's feet became all that mattered, as I thought about my own life and the lives of many of the people that I had sought to help over the years. I began to realise how easy it is to settle down into a routine of what is familiar and comfortable, forgetting that God has invested so much of Himself in equipping us to serve Him in our own generation.

Harris didn't stay at my feet for very long. As soon as puppies have had enough sleep they are up and doing, looking for action! Harris was no exception. One moment he had been sitting at my feet, the next he was all action looking for a game.

Gently God was showing me that He was wanting us to leave the comfort zone of our own security, come and sit at His feet and be prepared by Him for action - to faithfully do whatever He wanted us to do. The feet of Jesus is not a place of escape from responsibility - it is a place of preparation and equipping for what lies ahead.

I was beginning to understand what God was saying as He showed me that if we don't take time out to sit at His feet, our lives may never move out of the selfishness of our own comfort zone and could also be filled with exhausting and unproductive activity. When we spend precious time and resources on things that we are not meant to be doing and, sometimes, ungodly activites, our lives are unlikely to be fruitful and stress, anxiety and even burn-out may be the result.

I remembered the scripture from Isaiah where he reminds us that it is those "who wait on the Lord who will renew their strength". How can we fulfil the purposes of God if we fail to renew our spiritual strength by waiting on Him - sitting at His feet?

Harris was again asleep, recuperating from the latest bout of hectic activity. As I looked at the gentle swelling of his chest with each intake of breath, I sensed God's pleasure at the fact that Harris had arrived and He had got my attention!

I knew from that moment on that Harris was going to be no ordinary dog. God had a purpose for him beyond the confines of our family needs. He was going to have his own special work to do. The parables of Harris had started to be written!

Chapter 5
Harris Goes Deaf!

Harris soon expressed his desire to please his new owners by learning very quickly about where he could and could not make a mess on the kitchen floor. From the very beginning he was an incredibly clean dog. He always used the strategically placed newspapers and seemed to have no desire whatsoever to create a mess he would then have to walk in! House training was over almost before it had begun.

Like all puppies, Harris had the usual course of protective injections from the vet to protect him from all the catchable diseases that dogs can pass to one another. A little time has to pass for these to become fully effective and before it is safe to let him go outside where there might be the possibility of infection.

This intermediate period between leaving his mother and having the freedom to enjoy the open spaces was a valuable time of nurturing for our little pup. He soaked up a lot of love, but also demonstrated a considerable amount of independence. His motto could have been *Life is for Living!* For he sure did enjoy every aspect of life and lived it to the full - right from day one of his residence with us.

Labradors are natural retrievers. They are bred to carry things in their mouth, although the contents of waste-paper bins, toilet rolls, dirty socks and other suitably interesting items of clothing would not earn them any merit marks when out on a shoot! Nevertheless, for Harris it was great fun - especially when he got something in his mouth that we didn't want him to have. That was the signal for a glorious game of indoor chase.

He quickly learned the art of tantalising us by letting whatever it was he'd got hang loosely from his mouth, until we got within a few inches of snatching it from his jaws. At which critical moment he would take off in another direction, at a speed greater than we could match, leaving us sprawled across the furniture or the floor, helplessly laughing at our predicament as we saw the look of mischievous victory that literally smiled from his teeth, jaws and shiny black nose.

I know we shouldn't have laughed - that's not supposed to be good for his training. But he was laughing too, or so it seemed. In a funny sort of way these early adventures were very healing for us both. It was hard to get too bogged down by the seriousness and intensity of the pressures of work when there were interludes of such hilarity! And Harris loved them!

When we did begin to take him out and we met people who knew something about labradors, they would invariably comment, "What big paws he has". This was obviously of some significance to those who knew more than we did. "Never mind, he'll soon grow into them," said another.

It's only now that we are fully appreciating the wisdom of those early observers who obviously had a shrewd idea about just how big Harris was going to grow. He now stands head and shoulders above almost every other black labrador in the neighbourhood and has no difficulty in putting his huge paws on my shoulders, even though I stand six feet three tall. He is a big dog!

Although he's big, he is also ever so gentle. In fact, he's so gentle that our one year old grand-daughter could do anything she liked with him - and does! He shrugs off all the indignities he suffers with a protective wag of his tail, as if he actually knows what's expected of him.

Harris's first training lessons were in the safe confines of the kitchen. His very first lesson was learning to sit before being allowed to eat his meals. This was no problem to him. But the look he gave us spoke volumes and said something like, "I can't for the life of me understand why I have to sit before I eat, when everyone knows I can't eat out of my bowl while I'm still sitting down - but if you insist . . ."

He took the sitting lesson in his stride and was soon going a step further and lying down when told to "lie". Then on the command "sit up" he would immediately get up on his front paws, leaving his bottom firmly glued to the floor. He would sit, lie down and sit up again to perfection.

We were so proud of our little pup. In spite of his regular retrieving misdemeanours, as far as we were concerned Harris was turning out to be a very special little dog. But there was also just a little bit of pride slipping in at how wonderful we were at training him. Pride that was soon to be dealt a deserved blow!

As soon as the course of injections was complete and his period of confinement inside was over, I was keen to take him outside and start teaching him a few more lessons. I've learnt now that the experts wait a considerable period of time before real training begins, but I was keen to get going.

My first objective was to see him do the things outside that he was already doing so well in the kitchen. And then I planned to teach him to "sit and stay" until he was called.

Inside the kitchen he was perfect. Sit, lie down and sit-up were a regular part of his daily routine. So on his first visit to the large garden at the rear of our house, I started to take him through the routine as if he was still in the kitchen. He was so good at it inside the house that I expected instant obedience in the garden also. I was not prepared for what happened next!

I had carried Harris out of the kitchen and placed him gently down on the grass in the middle of the lawn. But the moment his paws touched the ground, his nose took over. The scents rising from the grass were just too much for him. He ran all over the place, totally consumed with the excitement of the many wonderful smells that were floating up his nostrils. All his labrador instincts were suddenly operating on full power.

Our garden borders on open fields and is regularly crossed by all sorts of wild life, ranging from hedge-hogs to foxes and ducks to the occasional visiting cat. What a wealth of labrador excitement there was for him at the end of his nose. Smells so faint that human beings could never detect them, were, for him, exploding into his senses. He was having such fun.

But then I reminded myself of what we were here for and started to get down to the serious business of outside training. I had a few treats and goodies in my pocket as rewards - the ones we had found he particularly enjoyed. They really helped the learning process along.

So, holding one of his favourite treats in my hand, I

gently called his name and said, "Harris, Sit". I might as well have told the moon to sit, for all Harris cared. His nose was back on the ground and he was having the most exciting day of his short life. All the instinctive memories that were built into his labrador mentality were coming alive. Sit? Treats? What's the point of silly things like that when there's so many exciting smells to investigate?

I will never know what particular smell was the most exciting, but I do know that even though I turned up the volume and, in the end, was shouting to the whole neighbourhood at the top of my voice, the words "HARRIS! SIT!" were having absolutely no effect whatsoever. Harris had suddenly gone totally deaf!

Fortunately, such deafness in young labradors is only a temporary condition, but even though he is now three years old, it is still a condition that overtakes him from time to time, especially when investigating a particularly juicy new smell.

The lesson I learned that day was very simple. When a labrador's nose gets turned on its ears get turned off! My pride in our obedient little pup took a heavy nosedive as I was totally unable to get Harris to listen to one word of command, let alone obey it. The treat in my hand was redundant - it held no attraction at all for a labrador pup with its nose switched on.

I was both frustrated with the lack of progress and entertained by his antics at the same time. As I watched him tear round the garden, I was trying to work out how to train him to be obedient outside as well as inside. It was then that I was once again surprised by what I recognised as the gentle voice of God, teaching me another lesson through this humbling experience.

It was as if God was saying to me, "Harris is just like my people and your kitchen is a bit like a church building. Inside the church the people do whatever the Minister tells them to do. When he says, "Stand up", they all stand up. When he says "Sit down" they all obediently sit down. In church they are just like Harris in the kitchen!

But when they get out into the world and start sniffing all the other exciting smells the world can offer them, they go deaf to me just like Harris went deaf to you.

They can be so consumed with following the scents of selfishness, and sometimes outright sin, that they are completely oblivious to my gentle voice warning them of dangers and calling them back to myself. The pursuit of sin always deafens the spirit."

As I walked back towards the house, I realised that I had failed to take Harris even one step further forward in his training, but that I had learnt a very important lesson and another parable had been added to the collection.

I was already thinking of circumstances when I could help others by telling the story to illustrate the teaching. But then the Lord gently spoke again and said, "Yes, you can use it to help others. But this is a lesson I want you to understand and learn first for yourself! There are many circumstances in life when it will be more important to hear my voice, than be consumed with the events and activities of the day. Always remember to listen - even when you have your nose close to the ground."

Suitably humbled I went inside and put the kettle on. I needed a cup of coffee. Harris followed me and without any need for a command sat down in front of me. His rich, brown eyes looked up - perhaps he was wondering what I was thinking about?!

Chapter 6
Harris and the Rhubarb Patch!

I love rhubarb! To me the flavour of rhubarb is one of the most delectable of all the flavours God created. Sweet young rhubarb, covered with hot, creamy custard - simply delicious! For sheer enjoyment it beats any of those *cordon bleu* restaurant puddings!

As far as I'm concerned you can keep those huge plates, decorated with fancy coloured, wiggly stripes, in the middle of which sits a tiny, edible work of art dusted down with icing sugar to make it look exotic, and which has cost you so much money it seems a sin to eat it! Give me a bowl of cold rhubarb and hot custard any day!

I've always enjoyed gardens but have never loved gardening. The process of keeping a garden tidy has to be repeated so often that unless you get personal enjoyment out of having a permanent vendetta with the dandelions, I think it is best left well alone and trusted to the expert vendetta-lovers.

Of course, I know that countless readers who get endless pleasure out of their garden will disagree with me, just as many others will not share my passion for rhubarb, considering it to be kid's food and the stuff of school dinners. Personally I'm far happier getting my recreational input doing things that don't need to be done all over again next week. But if somebody else does the work, that's a totally different story. For there's no better place on earth to relax and enjoy the beauties of God's creation than a much loved and well-tended garden.

Sadly, the permanent state of our garden reflects my lack of appreciation of having a weekly vendetta with the dandelions. So it was something of a traumatic experience for Fiona to suddenly discover her husband up to his neck in soil!

One day, shortly after Harris had become a member of the family, I made a visit to our local farm shop. All sorts of wonderful local procude can be purchased at this exciting country facility. Just in was a stock of magnificent rhubarb crowns - each in its own suitably big flower pot. "Ready for planting now" read the sign.

As I looked at these crowns, just pushing their heads above the surface of the soil, I could already taste the rhubarb. It had been years since I had picked rhubarb from my own garden and I suddenly caught the gardening bug or, at least, the gardening bug that specialises in home-grown rhubarb.

The rhubarb was having the effect of making me look like a fair imitation of Harris on a Sunday afternoon. As I carve the meat he sits patiently at my feet waiting for a corner off the Sunday joint, saliva pouring down his jowls until there is quite a pool of it on the kitchen floor. The only solution to the saliva flood is to give him a piece of meat quickly.

The only solution for my own developing saliva problem was to invest in some rhubarb crowns and take them home to plant in the garden. Harris and I arrived home together from the garden shop in triumph at the acquisition we had made.

As we appeared at the kitchen door, Harris was wagging his tail excitedly at whatever it was his master had bought. They sure looked like fun. But the look I got from Fi spoke volumes, "When are you going to find time to grow those". Actual words were unnecessary. Her look was incentive enough to prove that I, too, could be an expert at this gardening thing.

Never one to shrink from such a challenge, I soon had

my Wellington boots on and Harris and I disappeared together to the bottom of the garden where, close to the compost heap was a patch of waste land. Ideal for rhubarb, I thought.

But it did need some attention before the rhubarb could be planted. The weeds were well and truly in control of this particular piece of virgin soil. They were so bad that one could only assume this part of the garden had escaped the attention of gardening fiends for decades.

First I cleared the superficial growth, but I knew enough about real gardening to know that to get rid of the weeds one had to get the roots out as well. This required some serious digging. Soon I was totally pre-occupied with the task in hand.

At first, Harris seemed rather disinterested in the process of clearing the ground and went off to play. But before long he was back to investigate what I was doing. He's ever curious about things new and always wants to be with you when you are doing something interesting.

By this time I had dug quite a hole in the middle of the patch of ground and it was beginning to look as though growing rhubarb there could be a distinct possibility. I carried on digging for a while when, suddenly I was aware that Harris wasn't just watching what I was doing, he was joining in the experience.

Mercifully, Harris is not one of those dogs who is always digging holes in the garden to bury either his bones or anything else interesting he wants to hide for another day. He is not an instinctive hole digger, unlike some labradors I have known.

As far as I could remember, up to that point Harris had never dug a hole in his life. But he is a copier of whatever I'm doing, and he usually tries to join in the action and contribute to the operation in his own inimitable way.

On this occasion he had come right alongside me and was tackling the bit of ground next to the patch I had been digging. He rested his weight fairly and squarely on his widely spread back paws, his bottom high in the air, with his tail acting as a stabiliser, and set to work! His front paws began to move at an unbelievable speed, moving from front to back with a soil clearing action that an electrified giant mole would have been proud of!

Soil was going everywhere. I was amazed at what I was seeing. Finely powdered soil, weeds, roots, stones and anything his front paws turned over was being propelled through his rear legs at an extraordinary speed. At the same time his head and front paws were disappearing downward into an enormous and very well dug black hole!

Harris was oblivious to me and anything else that might have been going on. I called Fi over to come and see this whirlwind of a phenomenon. She looked on in amazement at what Harris was achieving. If only one could harness this amount of energy to do the whole of the garden, I thought! It was astonishing.

This proved to be another of those God moments when, as I looked on in disbelief, I became conscious of a gem of important truth taking shape in my mind. I was already asking the question to myself, "What makes Harris behave like this. He's never dug a hole before" when suddenly I had the answer to my silent question.

That insistent still small voice got through my defences to say, "He's only doing what his master is doing. And that's all I ask my people to do also. To do the same things that I did."

It was so simple, but so profound. It summed up the whole of the Christian life in one easy sentence. On two occasions Jesus had given Simon Peter some similar instructions, "Follow me!" It all sounded so right and so obvious. Man seems to have made religion so complicated with a host of traditions, rules and regulations.

Harris had progressed from sitting at his master's feet in the kitchen to doing what his master was doing out in the garden. That's exactly what God looks for in us, I thought, to sit at His feet, hear His voice and then go out and do what He is doing.

Harris was still digging when Fiona's voice interrupted my thoughts, "His hole is much bigger than yours!" I told her what I had been thinking and as she looked at the cavernous space still opening up beneath Harris she quietly responded, "Didn't Jesus say something about his disciples doing yet greater things?" We both needed a cup of coffee and as we headed for the kitchen Harris quickly followed, wondering what other adventures were in store. He was having such a good day!

Suitably refreshed I returned to finish the task and plant the rhubarb. Harris watched intently as I took the precious rhubarb crowns out of their pots and placed each one in a carefully prepared hole. He had put his head on one side - his preferred thinking position - obviously trying to work out why I would want to take the crowns out of the pots and bury them in the ground.

I was just burying the last one when Harris reached his conclusion, and having got there he was not slow to follow through with the action. He ran behind my back, enthusiastically disinterred the first rhubarb crown from its burial place and took off for three victory laps of honour around the garden with the whole crown placed firmly in his jaws like a baton in the 4 x 100m relay! He was so pleased with his prize. Now he understood exactly what I had been doing - providing him with a wonderful new game of course.

At times like this one should be angry and use the occasion to teach Harris a lesson. But we find it hard to be quite so tough and the humour of the situation always wins. Fi and I were helpless once again at the antics of our adventuresome labrador pup.

Eventually, just a little worse for wear, the traumatised rhubarb crown was recovered from the jaws of death and re-interred in the rhubarb patch. It lived to fight another day and the following year provided me with some of its fruit - perhaps as a thanksgiving for being rescued!

Harris has never again dug a hole in the garden, but, on reflection, neither have I. Perhaps there's a connection here? I've no doubt that if the gardening bug ever caught me again that Harris would be there to play his part in the ceremony!

Chapter 7
Harris Goes to School!

We were determined that not only would Harris be the best black labrador around, but that he would also be the best behaved. He was already growing up to be a tall, dark and handsome young dog and the time had come, we were told, to take his education a bit further and introduce him to the rigours of training in the company of other dogs.

We had already risked the occasional visit to the local pet shop where he seemed to have coped with various doggy encounters without any indication that he might want to have the first poodle he saw for breakfast, so we were hopeful that Puppy Class would be an enriching experience.

The pet shop ladies had said all the usual nice things about what a marvellous dog Harris was, as they leaned over the counter and dropped the occasional titbit in his mouth, making sure that Harris would want to come back here again. They 'ooed' and 'aahed' appropriately at everything from his fine head to his strong tail. We glowed in response, suitably priding ourselves on being such expert puppy selectors on that rather hasty visit to the breeding kennels.

Of course, we knew that it was in the very best interest of the pet shop owner's business to say exactly the same things about every new puppy that crossed their thresh-hold. People were unlikely to become life-long customers of the shop if the whole truth was spoken on every occasion! But we still believed what they said - probably because we wanted to believe it.

In reality every puppy is the most perfect dog in the world to its owners, so the pet shop ladies can hardly be accused of total deception - they were just agreeing with what the owners think! Anyway, it was the pet shop ladies who told us about the puppy classes and warmly commended these two lady trainers to us - one of whom was a professional trainer of labrador guide dogs for the blind. That was a good enough recommendation for us. So we booked him in and on the appointed day off we went, full of enthusiasm and expectancy.

The classes were held in a local village school hall. We were told to bring everything we might need for clearing up any unwanted mess. In reality this meant that Harris always got a very good walk before going to the class, to make sure he did everything that needed to be done in a safe place! He never let us down.

We were also told to bring suitable small treats to provide incentives for his training exercises. Clearly the class was going to be an exercise in bribery, without too much corruption we hoped!

The atmosphere of the first class was a cross between that of a mothers and toddlers group and an out of control circus in which all the different circus animals were in the ring at the same time. It didn't seem possible that any form of order could be brought to such a disorganised bunch of four-legged energy machines!

Owners were doing their best, in a slightly embarrassed sort of way, to pretend they didn't think their puppy was by far the best looking puppy in the class. The fact that all the owners were behaving similarly just goes to show how deceived we all were!

Harris had never encountered other dogs *en masse* before. He was completely at a loss as to what to do. His natural instinct was to give each one a good sniff in all the appropriate places. But how can you do this when you are also having to defend your integrity from the over-enthusiastic attentions of others in the class, whose motives seemed just a little less friendly? There were a collie, two spaniels, a white bull mastiff, an alsatian, several dogs whose lineage was certainly open to question and a number of other breeds, who must have behaved themselves too well to be noticed or remembered. About twenty dogs in all.

Our first instruction was "walk your dogs on the lead in a circle round the perimeter of the hall". Dutifully we all tried to tame our beasts and give the impression that we knew exactly what we were doing when, in reality, we were all petrified that our particular pet was going to embarrass us by its bad behaviour.

But the lady was a very good trainer and, amazingly, before very long she had us not only walking in a ring in the same direction, but each dog was put through its paces weaving in and out of all the other dogs while they sat dutifully down with their bottoms glued to the floor.

Then we were introduced to the gate. Each dog had to sit at the gate, allowing master or mistress to go through the gate first, before following on behind. It was clear that some of the dogs would always get everything right. It was equally clear that some of the dogs had so much independent spunk that doing exactly what they were told did not come totally naturally.

Harris was very much in this category. Life for him has always had to be lived at a pace considerably faster than is necessary for instant obedience! So, as the classes progressed it was obvious to us and, unfortunately, to the others, that Harris would probably have a few problems when it came to his examination at the end of the term.

Things weren't helped, either, by our own hectic travelling schedule which meant that a number of classes were inevitably missed, and on occasions he was taken to the class by someone else. That's our excuse for the fact that when the time for his exam eventually came, he was not as well prepared as all the other dogs. But we were hopeful that enough had gone into his labrador brain to help him scrape through - and I also had a secret plan!

There were ten different tests and each dog had to pass them all to get a certificate - fail one, and everything's failed! I knew Harris would be OK on most of the walking tests, both inside the hall and out on the street. He was very obedient at sitting on the kerb, when we reached the edge of the road, and he successfully managed what was his most difficult exercise, running close alongside me off the lead.

There was only one exercise to go. I was pretty sure that the visiting examiner had given him good marks on all the tests so far. In the final test I had to make him sit, off the lead, and then I had to walk a few yards away from him, turn round and face him and make him stay there for a whole minute before coming to collect his treat, when called. I was confident he would do this fine and I was already in my mind showing off his certificate!

But then Harris fell into a trap I had made for him. My secret plan failed! The test was timed for 6.30pm. Harris normally got fed at 5.00pm, so I decided that if I didn't feed him till after the test, he would be really hungry and be much more likely to do everything I asked him to do immediately, knowing that there was a treat waiting for him in my pocket.

The plan worked perfectly - until, that is, this final test. A minute is a long time for an enthusiastic dog to lie down and wait. But it is an even longer time for an enthusiastic and very hungry dog to have to wait knowing there is some food in his master's hands! As the seconds ticked by I could see him focussing on my hand where he knew the treat was.

The saliva of anticipation and hunger was already dripping from the side of his mouth. After twenty seconds he began to fidget. A hissed "stay" was enough to keep him there for another ten seconds, and a slightly louder instruction kept him there for a further ten.

Forty seconds had passed, twenty to go. I was beginning to get desperate - I knew the signs in Harris's body. Ripples of energy were appearing on his muscles. He was getting ready to break rank and run. Desperate prayers weren't answered and at forty-five seconds he could stay where he was no longer. Hadn't he waited for his treat long enough, he must have thought? He leapt forward to claim the reward that was waiting in my hand. His hunger had overtaken him.

The plan to keep him hungry had back-fired - he was so hungry that every treat was a desperately needed tasty morsel. If only I'd fed him before the class! It was all my fault. Harris was beaten by his own rumbling stomach, tripped up by hunger! He'd managed forty-five seconds. The kindly examiner gave him another chance at the same test, but this time he only managed forty seconds. Harris was too hungry to perform for anybody, even when a certificate depended on it!

At the end of the evening came the certificate ceremony. All the dogs that had survived the course were sitting in line next to their owners awaiting the judge's verdict. All except Harris were rewarded with their precious piece of paper, stating that they had passed the exam and achieved bronze standard. Proud owners went home wagging their imaginary tails, while dutifully obedient hounds trotted along beside them. Harris, however, was invited to re-take the course and try again next time.

He'd only failed on one test. I told him how sorry I was that I had kept him hungry and assured him that it was all my fault. I don't think he understood a word of what I was saying, but from the tone of my voice he did know he was still very much loved, and that even though he didn't have one of those silly bits of paper, he was still going to get a good dinner when he got home!

Even though I really wanted Harris to pass the exam, our love for him was not dependent on his achievements. There are many trials and tests that we all have to face at various stages of life. Some we sail through confidently, while at other times we make big mistakes and wonder how we will survive.

Fortunately God's love for us all is not dependent on our achievements. If we make mistakes God doesn't write us off - he still loves us and his arms are wide open to welcome us back, even when we have gone a long way from Him and made big mistakes.

The story Jesus told of the prodigal son tells it all. The father's arms were wide open to welcome him home, even though he had done many bad things and failed many of life's tests. As Harris and I went home that night, I knew my love for him was unchanged by the experience - I was quietly thankful that God's love is just the same.

As for Harris he had no idea what the fuss was all about as he curled up by the fire, totally secure and content at his master's feet!

Chapter 8
Harris's Misdemeanours

Well, we did set off to try and achieve 'the perfectly trained dog' - but so far we have failed miserably! We've now had Harris for three years, and although he is getting set in some of his doggy ways, perhaps there is still hope for progress with some of the others! As you will now be realising from other chapters, we have learnt a great deal from Harris's adventures and especially some of his misdemeanours!

From the beginning, like most pups, Harris set about chewing anything and everything in sight! But unlike most labradors, which seem to be heavily controlled by their stomachs, Harris has never been a particularly food orientated dog, so the kitchen waste bin has never been raided, nor has the larder where all his food is stored. But Harris did have a penchant for chewing shoes, cork, paper, plastic, wood and any household objects that were left lying around on the floor or at his eye level!

Sometimes we would watch him eyeing up a particular object and then look at us to see if we were looking. If we were he would be a little more cautious and might back off, but if he thought he could make a dash for the object, grab it and make off with his trophy before we could catch him, he would deliberately taunt us with his skill at always winning this particular game. I particularly remember the day he shredded the sports pages of the daily paper before I had managed to catch up with the football results!

Newspapers, cardboard boxes, serviettes, coasters, TV remote controls, pens, shoes, slippers and many other items were, as far as Harris was concerned, fair game! He especially loved sneaking under the table at meal time and pinching the serviettes from off the laps of our guests!

Ladies had to learn to leave their hand-bags firmly closed or risk the consequences of losing something precious or personal from deep inside! Any bag left open was vulnerable to an uninvited visit from Harris. One day, while we were all eating round the kitchen table, a quiet crunching could be heard in the distance.

It was a while before we realised Harris was no longer with us under the table, his normal mealtime catching position.

On investigation we discovered that my mother had unwisely left her bag open by the side of her chair. Harris's nose had fully investigated this treasure chest before carefully selecting her powder compact as his preferred trophy from the expedition. He then took it away for dismembering in a safe place.

Harris had us rolling with laughter on the day he proudly tried to burst through the kitchen door from the garden, having "retrieved" the wooden clothes prop! Of course it became well and truly stuck as he endeavoured to push it through the door. Undeterred, he eventually managed to bring the whole prop into the kitchen! On another day it was the bin lid and on yet another the watering can.

We will never know how he managed it, but on one day he bounded in and dropped a perfectly whole and undamaged duck egg gently at our feet. A few minutes later he brought another, but this time it was a broken one. He wagged his tail endlessly at his achievement, looking at us with a silly grin on his face, as much as to say "how about that then"? Then he ran off into the garden once more inviting us to join in the chase to the place where he proudly showed us the duck's nest where he had found a full clutch of eggs awaiting hatching. Sadly this particular clutch of duck eggs never reached maturity!

Harris's retrieving instincts knew no bounds and he constantly looked for anyone who would play his favourite games with him. We bought all kinds of doggy toys from the pet shop to try and keep him occupied - rope pulls, chews, balls, bones, squeaky toys, soft toys and anything you could name.

Harris had endless fun with them all, but his most precious toy proved to be the one that had cost us nothing - a large empty fizzy pop bottle. Not only did he love retrieving it, he also loved the noise it made as he and anyone who would play with him kicked it round the kitchen or the yard. He preferred playing the game indoors - it made more noise. He was, and is, an all action dog! Chasing Harris, especially when he had his bottle in his mouth, became his very favourite fun-time occupation.

On one famous occasion a wonderful game of 'bottle' was taking place round and round the kitchen. We all loved watching his agile manoeuvring to avoid being caught and losing his prize. Suddenly he leapt at the back of an armchair, at speed, using it as a springboard for a particularly effective dodging tactic.

Harris, however, was ignorant of Newton's laws of motion, which meant that as well as providing Harris with a spring-board to travel in one direction, the chair was propelled across the kitchen floor in the opposite direction. The chair's easy-roll casters were suddenly a liability as the it seemed to gather speed across the hard wooden floor, crashing dramatically into the glass front of the high-tech electric cooker!

The thick safety glass was shattered into a thousand tiny pieces instantly! The game came to an abrupt end, Harris fled out into the garden and we began to pick up the pieces and count the cost of entertaining Harris indoors. Insurance policies come in very useful at times like these!

In spite of having taught Harris early on how to sit and stay, we constantly struggled with getting him to obey the command 'come'. There did not seem to be anything in Harris's head to make him desire to come when we wanted him to, except what the books describe as a reward.

Having scoured all the books for an answer to the problem and taken him to puppy class, we got no other message from the experts other than to train him with his favourite treat as a reward! So, reward Harris we did!

We would speak the command 'Harris come' and reward him on his arrival. If Harris came to us when he had retrieved, we would reward him. However, in this respect, Harris was far cleverer than we were!

It never occurred to us at the beginning that this reward game was actually training him to be naughty! When he went off with a stolen 'toy' (such as a slipper or a shoe), we would give him the command 'leave', at which he would hold the object even tighter. We would then call him to come and come he did! As soon as he saw the reward, he would drop the toy immediately. We didn't realise it at the time, but in his doggy understanding, he saw this as being a fair exchange. Unwittingly we were teaching him to steal so that he could get another reward!

We ended up with a dog perfectly trained to pick up most objects around the house and then wait for us to call him to come for his reward! He thought it was a great game! Harris is a very intelligent dog who longs to be worked and exercised each day and this, to him, became the perfect way of exercising both himself and his owners!

Eventually, however, this aspect of his behaviour was getting to be a perfect nuisance. He aggravated not only us, but anyone who came to visit. Our house was being filled with cries of 'Harris, NO' and 'Harrrrrrrrris' and long sounds of 'aaaaaaaaaargh'! The dog responded to each of these with glee. He got the attention he was looking for, enjoyed the game and then had his reward!

The odd bit of paper did not seem to matter that much to us, but then there was the best pen or something much more valuable - a visitor's pair of spectacles, to which he gave a high speed circular tour of the garden, followed by three of us in hot pursuit! What were we to do?

We had no option (other than to reinforce bad behaviour with reward) but to chase him and grab him, at which point he would roll over, hiding his face under anything and everything until we were finally able to wrench the object from his mouth. I am sure that the real dog-training experts would have been horrified!

Again and again we tried every tactic we could think of to solve the problem. We tried bashing him on the nose, but this only served to make him more excitable. He would then tear round and round uncontrollably, outdoing all our efforts to catch or quieten him.

We tried keeping a lead tied on him in the house, so that we could catch him quickly whenever he grabbed something he shouldn't, but this only had the effect of teaching him to hate having his lead on! And this created a new problem, how do we get him to sit, while his lead is being put on for his legitimate walks, when he sees his lead as a controlling threat? The lead meant restraint and so he then wanted to avoid any sight of it. The reward remained the only exchange for good behaviour that Harris recognised, but alongside rewarding him, his bad behaviour was increasing steadily!

Eventually, we hit on the solution, we had to ignore him! He had learned to love the instant attention that grabbing an item of treasure always brought. Hard as it was, we had to train ourselves not to react with a guttural scream when he grabbed the TV controls or anything else precious.

The sight of sometimes three or four adults chasing a very large black lab around a smallish lounge, ducking and diving between all the furniture and eventually landing up on top of each other and Harris, had ceased to amuse us! This was especially true when these antics occurred during visits from important guests! Introducing them to our four footed friend certainly produced a whole new way of helping people to get to know us. Harris left no room for superficial relationships!

But ignoring Harris was not easy. Many times, we had to stifle our laughter as much as our yelling. Perhaps it was his growing older, rather than our new tactics which began to bring calm to him, but eventually he began to understand the difference between his toys and our possessions! His naughtiest games began to diminish in regularity and today we can say that, mostly, he is very good at not retrieving household items.

However, he still has times when he cannot resist picking up a shoe or a slipper which, thankfully, he no long chews to bits. He only occasionally pinches the serviettes from our laps during mealtimes and only yet more occasionally runs off with the TV controls or a pen. It was a relief when, at the age of around two and a half, Harris began to respond to us lifting a magazine over his head as a threat. We could then speak the word 'drop' and he would do so, which brought us a measure of control and success in handling the problem.

This was an invaluable lesson for life today. In giving so much attention to his bad behaviour, we had escalated the problem. In our futile efforts to manage one problem, we had created another. Human nature and doggy nature both need some 'fear' deterrent (not cruel punishment) in order to help control behaviour. The consequences of sin are real and need to be learnt. For Harris, ignoring him, together with the occasional threat of punishment, had become a significant deterrent. One thing labradors cannot stand is being ignored. Bad behaviour is unpleasant to live with and has to be dealt with - in both dogs and humans.

We learnt so much about God and His principles through Harris. It was not so bad when he managed to run off with the odd serviette, or even perhaps a pen or a coaster but when he quietly stole a salesman's cheque-book from his briefcase, and began to chew it to pieces under the very table on which the salesman was laying out his plans for a possible new conservatory, it became rather embarrassing to say the least!

When this was discovered we hastily ushered Harris outside. We got the impression that the salesman's bland smile rather covered the fact that he could have murdered Harris! But being a salesman, his desire to sell the goods meant that he could say nothing.

Even this was not so bad as the day Harris chewed up our friend's most expensive and favourite leather court shoe! She was chatting away animatedly and, unknown to us, had casually kicked off her shoes under the table without any thought as to who was lying in wait below. Harris was in heaven as he gradually reduced this expensive leather shoe from being a work of art to something approaching scrap leather. We understand that Harris is still on her forgiveness list for this particularly grievous sin!

The worst of the worst came when in an unsuspecting moment, Harris managed to steal another friend's palm-top computer. Not being soft and yielding like a stuffed toy or a real duck, in a flash of time he had sunk his teeth into the controls and rendered this high-tech toy completely useless. Fortunately the insurance enabled him to buy a better model for the same price, so Harris was doubly forgiven!

These were the moments when we felt like screaming unrepeatable words at the dog. In particular, there were times when we thought we had done the wrong thing in getting him in the first place. When things were really bad, "this dog will have to go" became our litany. We thought we would have to take him back to the kennels or give him away!

We hit our wits end on several occasions during those early days with Harris. However, when love is the bottom line one always relents! One look from those almond shaped deep brown eyes, the rolling over onto the tummy waiting for it to be tickled, the nudging up to you for affection, the warm silky coat waiting for a stroke and a hundred and one other endearing features, all serve to melt the heart and release forgiveness into the relationship. And with forgiveness comes a further resolve to continue the training and partnership together. How glad we are that we persevered.

It was on one of those days that Harris had tried our patience to the limits, that I became acutely aware of one aspect of the nature and character of our God. When

God created mankind and had given him all this world to enjoy and live in and take care of, He must have looked sadly at the equivalent of Harris's misdemeanours and felt like we did. At times He must have wanted to finish the relationship altogether, do away with us and start again. How incredibly patient our God is that He allows us to continually mess things up, to break His laws, to steal precious things, desecrate them and even render them useless without exhausting the limits of His love.

I was visiting a very lovely seaside town in Britain not so long ago, when I was overcome with righteous anger by a monstrosity of a building - a huge steel framed concrete cube, which had been placed right on the edge of the sea-shore, in a place which prevented people from being able to see the view or the sea.

The building was a massive new cinema. There were no windows for obvious reasons. The simple beauty of nature, which no man could create and which God had provided for free, had been obliterated by a building whose object was to attract thousands to pay money for the artificiality of screen movies.

As I looked at this I shook my head in disbelief that the local authorities in one of the most lovely seaside places in Britain today, should have allowed this massive monstrosity to obscure such a large section of the seashore. Man has really messed it up. I became acutely aware of the love of God and of how big His mercy and His grace must be towards us when you consider the extent of messing up mankind has done.

On the rare occasions when Harris completely messed up the house, chewed furniture, muddied the carpet and kitchen, and I am left having to clear it all up, I think of how God must feel. I clear up Harris's mess simply because we love having a dog and this is part of the relationship.

I feel the same awareness of God's love, which is so great for us that even when we mess it up, which we constantly do, He does not do away with us or wipe us off as useless. But His mercy is tender and patient towards us. He simply waits for us to look to Him again. He asks for our trust and our willingness to follow Him. He does not force us, but waits for us to come to Him.

How similar is the relationship between a dog and his owner. The joy of having a dog is that the dog recognises you as His owner, freely wants to be with you, trusts you, follows you and loves to partner and adventure with you.

This chapter has been about the love, mercy and grace of God which, while we are sinners is extended towards us because He loves us, wants to forgive us and wants us to learn to watch Him and trust Him more, so that He can get the best from us and allow us to enjoy the best He has to give. Handling Harris has helped us enormously to understand the mercy in God's heart.

Chapter 9
Harris Gets Lost!

In his early days we soon found out how much Harris enjoyed walks along the towpath of the local canal. He just loved the canal environment. So many things to sniff and enjoy. So many exciting adventures for a young dog to savour. So many new things to experience and enjoy. So much water to experiment with!

Three years later, the canal is still his favourite walking territory. Only now he jumps in and out of the canal retrieving anything that is floating on the surface and burrowing his head in the reeds as if looking for some game bird to retrieve for his master. All great fun and wonderful entertainment for him and us. He is always making us laugh with his expressions of surprise when he comes across something he has never seen or experienced before.

One day, when he was running as usual along the towpath, he put his head in a clump of grass and came face to face with a duck sitting firmly on her clutch of eggs. She had no intention of moving whatsoever, even for the likes of a marauding labrador. Guarding her eggs was more important than her life.

Harris put his nose very close, but then retreated just enough to stare at her. He then lay down nearby and marked the spot with his nose pointing straight at the nest. But never once did he go close enough to disturb the duck in her God-given mission to protect the next generation. It was as if there was an unwritten understanding and mutual respect between them.

If the duck had been shot down and was lying dead in the grass, she would have been fair game for a labrador and that would have been a very different story. Only very recently did I have to use all my strength on the lead to stop Harris retrieving a dead duck from the canal which had been there a very long time and was distinctly unsavoury!

On another occasion he encountered a swan guarding six nearly adult cygnets. He was deeply shocked to discover that the unwritten law that had prevailed when facing a duck in its nest did not apply to a swan guarding its cygnets! The swan let its intentions be known in no uncertain terms with loud hisses which threatened a devastating physical attack if Harris had dared to jump in the water and go any nearer to the brood.

Pssssssssssssssssssssssssssssssssssttttttttttttthhhhhhhhh was not a word that was in Harris's vocabulary up to that point! We had to pull him away on his lead very quickly to avoid a full confrontation, knowing just how dangerous an adult swan can sometimes be.

Without Harris we would never have had the daily exercise that his twice a day walk requires. And neither would we have found out what a happy hunting ground it is in the autumn, when the wild blackberries are at their best and the hedgerows are bursting with fruit just crying out to be picked. Pockets stuffed with polythene bags became an essential constituent of autumn adventures by the canal.

Picking blackberries, however, is something which Harris totally fails to appreciate. Why he should have to sit and wait so long while his owners "sniff" the hedgerow is always beyond his understanding. When Harris has extracted the maximum benefit from each of his own hedgerow sniffs, he always wants to move on to the next sniff and the next one and the next! But wait he has to, while his owners "sniff" their favourite bit of the hedgerow and fill the polythene bags with delicious autumn fruits, soon to become the stuffing of blackberry and apple pies.

These days we always keep Harris on a lead, even along the canal where there is no traffic. He has one of those long expanding leads which give him a lot of liberty to enjoy himself, while at the same time giving us the capacity to rein him in when necessary. We would love to let him off completely, but his hunting instinct has proved too strong for his own safety.

When he was young though, we thought differently. Most days we would slip the lead from his neck and let him adventure along the towpath to his heart's content. He made lots of friends with his ever-wagging tail and ever-curious face. He would run off adventuring, then run back to join us for a few minutes before running off again to claim a doggy treat which we gave him every time he came back to us, especially when we had called him. He was having such fun.

One day he was doing just this. It was a winter's evening in December and the night was closing in fast. Within half an hour it would be dark. He had run off and come back to me again as usual on several occasions when, suddenly, I was overtaken on the towpath by a runner who had come up silently behind me. He was past me in seconds.

We were both taken aback by the experience, for neither of us had seen or heard the runner until he was right upon us. Harris looked at me, looked at the runner, looked at me again and then, his mind made up, he had decided to give chase and was off! As soon as he felt the excitement of his legs carrying him at speed along the towpath, the fun of the chase overtook his desire to stay close to his master.

I thought he would soon turn round, so I let him run a short distance, before calling his name gently. He totally ignored me. I then called out much more loudly, Harrrrrrrrriiiiiiiiissssssssssssssssssssssssss! He was already at least sixty yards or so ahead of me and the runner was disappearing round the next bend in the canal.

He heard my voice, hesitated for a moment, stopped for a second, looked round at me, looked again at the disappearing heels of the runner, looked back at me once more and then, once again, he was off. This time there was no stopping him.

He was going to show that runner what he was made of! The chase was on. You could almost hear him thinking, even at that distance, that if you want a race, then you won't beat me.

Now he was really away and nothing was going to stop him. He was round that bend in the canal in a flash and after his prey as fast as his four young legs would carry him, now followed by me in full chase also. But there was probably forty years between me and the age of the young runner and I soon realised that my wind capacity was not what it was when I was running for my college forty years earlier!

I fully expected that by the time I turned the bend in the canal, however, that I would see a happy Harris, having enjoyed a bit of exercise, coming trotting contentedly back to his master. But by the time I could see round the bend for myself, there was neither sight nor sound of our precious pup or the runner. Both had already disappeared from sight.

By now I was panicking, panting and praying all at the same time. "O Lord, guard Harris" was panted out between deep breaths, each of which at that stage seemed as though it might be my last! I had visions of being found on the towpath having had a heart attack and Harris joining a road at one of the bridges and being run over.

It was a dreadful moment. I was berating myself for ever having let him off the lead, still running as fast as I could to try and catch him, praying staccato prayers of "O God help" and wondering how I would tell Fi that he had gone.

It was only then that I fully realised how attached I had become to our one year old, four legged addition to the family. I was already thinking of life without Harris and imagining his trusting face looking up at me from the hearthrug beside the fire. Already in my mind I had enlarged the best pictures of him to remind us of what a lovely dog he had been and was planning how I would cope with life without Harris. And Harris is only a dog!

I then began to feel guilty about having such feelings about a labrador, when there are countless people every day who have to come to terms with much greater traumas affecting human members of their families.

Having stuffed the guilt somewhere in my emotions, I then set about serious prayer for Harris and his safety, as well as plan a strategy for finding him. I was now a long way from where I had parked the car. I had no idea whether Harris was still running or had left the canal at some point - what was certainly clear was that I did not have the puff to keep running after him.

He couldn't be behind me along the canal, so there was no point in going back. I left the towpath at the next bridge and ran, walked, trotted, puffing and panting all the way, along the road, covering the two or more miles back to where I had parked the car as fast as I was capable of. I was well and truly done for, when I finally put the key in the lock and collapsed into the driver's seat.

By now it was dark and I realised that the chances of finding a black dog on a black winter's night were getting less and less. I put my foot down and drove home as quickly as I could. I blurted out to Fi what had happened, told her to ring the police and inform them just in case someone might ring in with his details. Our name and phone number were on Harris's collar.

I then jumped back in the car and was off again to drive the many lanes that criss-cross the countryside in vain hope of picking up the reflection of his eyes in the headlights. The more I drove the more despairing I became. Rather forlornly I asked some farmers to look out for him and not to shoot him if they saw him in a field with some sheep.

Part of my panic and fear stemmed from what had happened to a previous black labrador, who had been shot dead by an unfriendly and thoughtless farmer, just because he was in a the same field as some sheep.

On that occasion I had had to exhume the body of our pet dog from where it had been hastily buried by a very guilty farmer. I could still sense the emotion of that awful day as I dug into the soil and identified the dog who had been a family pet for seven years. Anger could never bring a dead dog back and on that occasion I not only had to do some physical digging but had to dig deep into the wells of forgiveness as well. I had no wish for a repeat performance.

As the emotions of the earlier experience surfaced, the depth of my prayer for Harris intensified. An hour later I returned home. I hadn't found him. No-one had seen him. He was gone.

It was now pitch black outside. The winter's night had totally enveloped our farmhouse and it seemed as though the cold of winter was coming inside. Harris's bowl of food was untouched and there was no happy little patter of feet around our ankles as Fiona dished out our evening meal. But neither of us wanted to eat.

I rang the police again. No, no-one had reported a missing dog and they had no report of any accidents either. At least the latter was a glimmer of good news.

We made some phone calls asking people to pray and set about waiting. Fiona and I held each other in the kitchen, wondering if we would ever see Harris again. It seemed as though an eternity had passed when suddenly the phone rang.

An unknown voice on the other end of the phone said, "Have you lost a dog?" I have no idea what I said in response, for at this stage I had no idea whether they were reporting Harris dead or alive. The voice went on, "We've got him here, he's frightened, but he's OK. He was nearly run over and I saw it happen in my headlights. I saw he was a proper dog so I stopped and got him in my van. He was hiding in the hedge." I was crying and unable to speak with emotion and relief. I could hardly write down the address where he was, but get it down I did.

As Fi and I ran towards the car to go and get him, we remembered it was Christmas. What could we take to say thank you? We grabbed a big tin of chocolates we'd bought for a friend and a bottle of sherry we'd bought for someone else and were off.

It was an awfully emotional moment when we were re-united with Harris, who was still inside the man's van when we got to his house. His children really appreciated the chocolates and he was grateful for the sherry, but we were unbelievably relieved and thrilled to have our Harris back.

We must have said all sorts of gibberishly silly things to Harris as we took him home that night. He had been naughty in running off, but that was the farthest thing from our thoughts, as we fed and stroked him in front of the fire. We were just so thrilled that he was home again, safe and sound. Our prayers of thanks were not silent prayers that night. We were glad to tell God just how grateful we were!

I will never forget the intense sense of pain and grief I experienced when I saw Harris make that final decision to give chase to the runner and ignore his master's voice. The pain was so deep and real only because of the love that we had for Harris. Without love there would have been no pain.

As I have thought again about that incident, I have realised afresh how much it must have hurt God to see the whole of mankind choose to ignore His voice - a choice that resulted in evil being given access to the world God had made.

My pain and grief was absolutely nothing when compared with the sheer agony that God must have gone through - an agony that was only made real by the depth of His love for the world and His ultimate creation, the human race. And then I realised how every time human beings reinforce that choice, by continuing to do their own thing and ignoring the voice of God within their conscience, they must increase the pain in God's heart.

The concern of the van driver who saw Harris in his headlights and stopped to rescue him reflects the fact that God loved the world so much he sent His only Son to rescue those who would turn to Him. Jesus is referred to in Scripture as the Light of the World. Wherever His light shines darkness is overcome and when we are caught in the searchlight of His love we have a choice over whether or not we respond to His love and allow Him to rescue us.

The joy we experienced as we comforted each other with Harris by the fireside, is nothing compared with the sheer joy there must be in God's heart over each and every person who does turn back to God and receives Jesus as His Saviour.

Just as we held no anger with Harris for the mistake he made in running off, God does not hold our sin against us. It is completely covered by what Jesus did for us on the cross. All we need to do to receive His forgiveness, and know His love, is to come home to the place we really belong - right in the centre of His love, learning again to sit at His feet, listen to His voice and make the right choices when temptations come rushing up on us in the business and busy-ness of life.

Not surprisingly, we have never let Harris off the lead again along the canal. We are too concerned for his safety to risk letting him go where he likes. If only Harris had learned to remain within the security of calling distance, he could have had so much more freedom!

Without his collar and identity disc we may never have got Harris back. But one day, when he had been jumping in and out of the canal on his extending lead and choker chain, his neck collar must have come off in the water and he came home having lost both his red collar and his disc.

We realised then that even a good collar can come off, so we had Harris micro-chipped, so that if he ever got lost again, and even if he had also lost his collar and disc, whoever found him could readily have him identified with the help of the police or a local vet. All his identification data is contained within the chip.

A few days after losing his collar the telephone rang again. This time from one of the people who permanently live on long-boats on the canal. He had found the collar and disc in the reeds. Harris and I needed little excuse to go and make the man's acquaintance and thank him for his kindness. We were invited aboard and were glad to build relationship with these lovely people. Harris has made us many friends!

The purpose of both the disc and the micro-chip are to provide for Harris's safety, by making sure that anyone can quickly find out who he belongs to. Many people today are full of fears, but someone who has found Jesus to be their Saviour need never fear - for their lives have been marked by Him as belonging to God for eternity.

Chapter 10
Harris Finds Mr. Jinks!

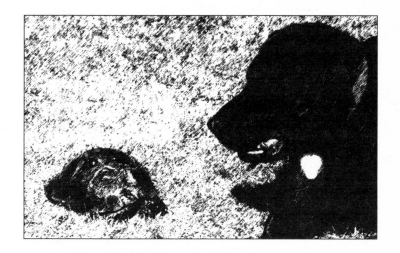

Mr. Jinks is the oldest member of the family. No-one knows exactly how old he is, but he is probably well over a hundred! He is large, well armoured and very determined. He also sleeps extensively - usually from October till April - and when he wakes up he eats dandelion flowers till there are no more!

I was brought up in Lancashire, in the north of England. But at the age of nine the whole family left our beloved Blackburn and moved south to Cheam in Surrey. Children quickly make friends with other children, so before long I was in and out of the homes of other kids in the road doing all the things that boys brought up in the fifties would enjoy doing.

One day I came home with a new friend under my arm. I'd always wanted a pet, although I cannot consciously remember thinking that a tortoise would be top of my wants list. For various family reasons a dog was out of the question, so when Nicholas offered me one of his tortoises I didn't hesitate to accept.

I carefully lifted Oswald up to carry him the few hundred yards to our garden, his new home. I held him tight in my two hands, with his head pointing away from me, and his feet kicking hard for all they were worth to try and find some *terra firma*. Being ignorant of such things, it never occurred to me that a frightened tortoise that has recently woken up from a long sleep was able to evacuate its bowels of both liquids and solids in one large, energetic self-defensive action!

Oswald can consider himself fortunate that I did not drop him instantly when he suddenly jettisoned his winter cargo all over the front of my trousers on the way home! He soon became familiar with our garden and my father quickly discovered that tortoises enjoy eating most of the things that he had specially planted.

There was another family in the road, who also had a tortoise, and one day, just before they moved house, I was asked if Oswald wanted a friend and I was introduced to Mr. Jinks, the name by which he had been known throughout his history of living with three separate families. We calculated he must have been well over fifty years old in nineteen fifty-three.

I can hardly say it was love at first sight, but caring for two tortoises did not seem to be excessively arduous, so Mr. Jinks joined the family also. We never knew what sex either of them were, but no eggs were ever laid so we are assuming that whatever it was they must have been the same.

Oswald was about nine inches long, but Mr. Jinks was significantly larger and altogether much more aggressive. When he wanted to go somewhere he would just plough through whatever obstacle was in his way with the ease of a tank being deployed in a field of corn. We soon found also that he was something of an escapologist.

Both tortoises had the run of the garden and on most evenings, just before dusk, they could be seen trudging back to the hut they shared from wherever in the garden they had been eating or sunning themselves. There was a strict order of protocol about entry to the hut - Mr.Jinks had to be in first. And if Oswald had made it home before Mr. Jinks, and dared to go in first, then there was an almighty tortoise scuffle until Oswald exited from the hut, let Mr. Jinks in and then brought up the rear.

Occasionally one or the other of the tortoises would be missing when we checked the hut last thing at night. Being cold-blooded creatures, if the temperature drops suddenly they can run out of energy to get back home, so they simply camp wherever it is they were when the temperature dropped.

On many a night members of the family could be seen out in the garden with a torch, hunting for the missing beasts. We had to find them, because on occasions their adventurous spirit and all round armoured protection would take them through gaps in the fence to adjacent gardens, where the neighbours were less than appreciative of a marauding tortoise that had the capacity to demolish a bed full of tasty plants in no time!

Once Mr. Jinks was picked up by some American tourists as he headed towards the bus stop on the main road. Fortunately they asked one of our neighbours if they knew where he belonged. They did and Mr. Jinks was returned home, almost kicking and screaming at having been discovered, but none the worse for his adventure!

It's easy to think of tortoises as being slow moving creatures, as epitomised by Aesop in his fable of the tortoise and the hare. But take your eye off them for a moment and it seems as though they can cover a remarkable expanse of ground in a very short time. I fully understand why the careless hare lost the race in Aesop's story!

Fifty years have passed since Mr. Jinks first arrived and started to do his armoured tank impressions in my childhood garden. Oswald, sadly, fell over on his back about twenty five years ago and never recovered from having been fried all day by the hot sun - not even a touch of brandy could kick start the old boy (girl?) into life.

But Mr. Jinks, it seems, is destined to go on almost for ever, having several times been found on his back without any apparent consequences. He long since sailed past his 100th birthday and is heading for something like his 110th or 120th birthday. These days tortoises are a rare breed and worth a lot of money, not that Mr. Jinks is aware of his increasing value or that we are thinking of cashing in on the investment!

Anyway, all of this is by way of introduction to the day Mr. Jinks got lost. He now lives in a substantial pen in the garden. Having hunted for him on many occasions over the years, sometimes almost despairingly, I decided that as I got older, looking after him had to be made easier - especially as we often had other people living in the house looking after the livestock.

When Harris came on the scene we introduced him to Mr. Jinks at an early age. All fears that Harris would treat Mr. Jinks as a mobile bone and chew him to shreds were quickly dispensed with. Harris almost seemed fond of the old boy and would sniff him contentedly without ever trying to grab his head, turn him over or gnaw his shell. It seemed as though Harris had even learned his name, for when you mentioned the tortoise's name, he would put his head on one side, run to the pen and give Mr. Jinks a good sniff.

Occasionally we would give Mr. Jinks some exercise by releasing him from the pen and giving him the run of the garden for a while. This was always under close supervision though, for if Mr. Jinks once got into the adjacent fields he would probably be gone for ever. On several occasions we thought he had disappeared when we took our eye off him for a moment, or went inside to make a quick cup of tea.

But then came the day when he really had disappeared. Maybe there had been a phone call while making the cup of tea, or something else had distracted our attention. Whatever it was, we suddenly realised Mr. Jinks had gone. He was nowhere to be seen and so the search began for the hundred year old tortoise. It was towards evening and even though we looked absolutely everywhere, he was nowhere to be found.

Early in Harris's life we had taught him a little game by hiding a doggy treat under one of the cushions on the sofa. On the word "find" he would energetically lift all the cushions with his nose and sniff out the seat which contained the hidden treasure. His nose never failed to find the treat. When I sniffed a piece of the biscuit it was, to me, totally without smell. But to Harris's sensitive nose even a dry biscuit was no problem!

We had never thought of using Harris as a 'search and rescue' dog before, but someone had the idea of recruiting Harris to join in the search for Mr. Jinks. So the command was given, "Find Jinks."

We watched in stunned amazement as Harris got to work. He went straight to the pen, put his head to the ground and with the point of his wet, black nose never more than a hair's breadth from the grass, he sniffed his way across the lawn at quite a speed, going this way and then that way, obviously following what, to him, was a very strong scent. Then, in the far corner of the garden he excitedly began to burrow in the bushes with his head, while at the other end his tail was triumphantly wagging at an accelerated speed, signalling his achievement.

It had taken Harris no more than thirty seconds to find Mr. Jinks. He got a very generous reward that night as I lifted Mr. Jinks out of the bushes, under which he was half buried, and returned him to the safety of the box inside his pen. On the way I lifted Mr. Jinks to my nose and took a sharp intake of breath. I could smell nothing! I was beginning to appreciate just how sensitive is the nose of a black labrador.

Since then we have felt a little more confident about giving Mr. Jinks a run in the garden, knowing that in the event of an emergency we had our own four-legged rescue service! Harris loves to perform for visitors. He has never failed to find the tortoise on the command "Find Jinks". There is now nowhere Mr. Jinks can hide without us knowing that he can be found - thanks to Harris.

I don't think the Psalmist David ever had a pet tortoise, but several times he expressed the thought that there is nowhere he can go and nothing he can do that God doesn't know about. He always knows where we are. Even when we may think we are lost God knows where we are. There is never a moment when we might want to cry out to God for help and God doesn't know where we are.

Harris's nose might be very sensitive. But God's understanding and God's knowledge never fail. He is always there when we need him. Even if we have tried to go our own way and run a long way from him, he has promised to hear our cry when we turn to him. When Harris never fails to find Mr. Jinks, it always reminds me of the security there is in God for those who are willing to trust Him.

Chapter 11
Harris Goes to Harris!

After the decision had been made to get Harris, we had a few days to think about his name before returning to the kennels to claim our pup on my birthday, when he was nine weeks old.

During those few days we had a virtually continuous conversation about what his name was going to be. It seemed as though we had exhausted every doggy possibility from Sam to Buster, but none seemed to fit the face of our pup with his identifying spot of pink nail varnish.

The day before we were to collect him we were driving home from work and conversation casually turned to our annual summer holidays in Scotland on the Isle of Harris. Simultaneously we looked at each other and blurted the name out. Harris! His name is Harris!!

The name had a suitably male, distinguished and distinctive ring about it. Instantly we knew it was the right name for our pup. We had had so many happy holidays on that remote Hebridean island. Every time we called his name we would be reminded of the fun and adventures that the family had enjoyed there. So Harris he became.

Harris and Lewis are two parts of the same island in the Outer Hebrides of Scotland. Some time after we got Harris we were walking along the towpath of the canal and met a man who was admiring Harris because he looked so like his cousin's dog.

As the conversation went on and we compared notes, we realised that both dogs must have come from the same breeding kennels and then from the dates when the pups were collected we deduced that it was most likely that Harris was a brother of his cousin's dog, from the very same litter. But then we discovered the most amazing coincidence - this other dog was called Lewis! So out of the one litter two dogs had been independently named after the two different parts of the same Hebridean island!

Harris soon learned his name and we talked regularly

of one day taking him to the island after which he was named. He was nearly two years old when we finally made the pilgrimage with Harris on board.

The Isle of Harris is reached by either a flight to Stornoway (in Lewis) or by road. By road the journey is long and beautiful - through wild Glencoe to Fort William, then across to Loch Duich via the mountains known as the five sisters of Kintail, past Scotland's most famous and picturesque island castle, Eilean Donan, and then across the new bridge to Skye from Kyle of Lochalsh. And finally from there to Uig, at the northern tip of the Isle of Skye, to await the Caledonian Macbrayne ferry which has carried visitors to the outer isles for generations.

Harris is completely at home in the car. It's his second home. He loved the journey and was not at all bothered when the car suddenly descended into the belly of the ferryboat for the journey to Tarbert on the Isle of Harris. Not for him a voyage across the sea locked in the hold though - he wanted to see what was going on. He was quickly up the steep stairways, and along the corridors to the lounge, where he took up guard duty in a suitably prominent place to receive the admiring glances of every dog-lover that passed by.

As the ship slipped its moorings with a loud blast on its hooter, you would have thought Harris had done the journey a hundred times. He was going "home" - or at least to the land he was named after! He soon had a small gang of children around him wanting to give him a stroke and talk to him. They were local children from Harris who were very excited to discover the dog was called after their island.

It seemed quite a significant moment when Harris first put his paws down on the island. Before long we were running with him along one of the glorious beaches on the west side of the island, where he had his first encounter with the Atlantic ocean. He had never seen waves before. Most of his previous water experience was by the side of the motionless canal.

We laughed as he worked out what to do with this moving water which was constantly attacking him every time he tried to go for a paddle. His way of dealing with this liquid enemy was to wait till the wave was almost on him and then j-U-M-p, as the wave would pass safely under him. That was fine for the smaller waves, but when he encountered some bigger waves he had to pluck up the courage to plough through them. He didn't seem to be bothered by the Atlantic's cold temperature.

The beach was sheer heaven for him. We soon discovered how much he enjoyed digging in the sand, but only when someone else was digging with him! As usual, with Harris, he just loved to copy whatever we were doing. Even though we were rather older than most beach diggers, we couldn't resist starting to dig, just to watch Harris showing us how to do it properly!

Instead of digging a hole within the limitations of the rhubarb patch - he was now digging on a beach with an unlimited amount of sand, all of which, it seemed, needed to be dug! He set about it with an extraordinary bout of energy and effectiveness.

It was on the island, however, that Harris discovered sheep. As far as he was concerned these were white dogs, about the same size as himself and, surely, they would want to play a game of chase. It was clear that when we took him amongst the sheep on his extending lead that they had an unusual interest for him. He strained at the leash with the eager anticipation of a greyhound waiting for the arrival of the hare.

We thought of letting him off the lead, thinking how much he would enjoy the freedom of running along the beach, up and down the sand dunes and over the headlands, but discretion, concern for the sheep and our desire to maintain good relationships with the local shepherds kept us from risking it.

Always at the back of our mind was the experience of losing him when he followed the runner along the canal. Not that there were many Hebridean runners, but who knows how far he would run in the search for adventure and would we ever see him again? We longed to give him his freedom, but realised that freedom without the ability to provide restraint was too dangerous - even for Harris on Harris - as we were about to discover.

The grounds around the house we stay at in Harris are well fenced. So Harris is perfectly safe to run wherever he likes within the fence line. At night he would sit with his head held high watching the sheep on the other side of the fence as the shepherd and his dogs brought the flock together and then played expert games with them.

The sheepdogs moved like grease lightning at the various sounds of the shepherd's whistle. Harris was totally mesmerised as the sheep would go this way, then that way, as if by magic. Then one dog would separate out a group of sheep into one corner of the field and then another would do the same in another part of the field. He couldn't take his eyes off the nightly performance as he watched the shepherd training a young sheepdog for a lifetime of keeping the sheep safe.

He would sit there for ages taking it all in. His whole body bristling with readiness, as if he was just waiting for his turn to show everyone what he could do with those sheep. He'd show those sheepdogs what a labrador is made of. Only when the show was finally over would he desert his watching position and come back inside. He would then lie on the carpet, the tension of the moment would dissipate and he would fall fast asleep, obviously dreaming deeply of sheep, judging by the twitches and grunts which came from his snoring body.

During the day Harris would constantly be alert to what the sheep were doing in the field beyond his fence. Then, one day, a workman opened the gate that led down to the beach and left it unguarded for only a few seconds. Harris is a fast runner and he had clearly been awaiting his opportunity to play tag with all those white dogs which tantalisingly were free to go wherever they

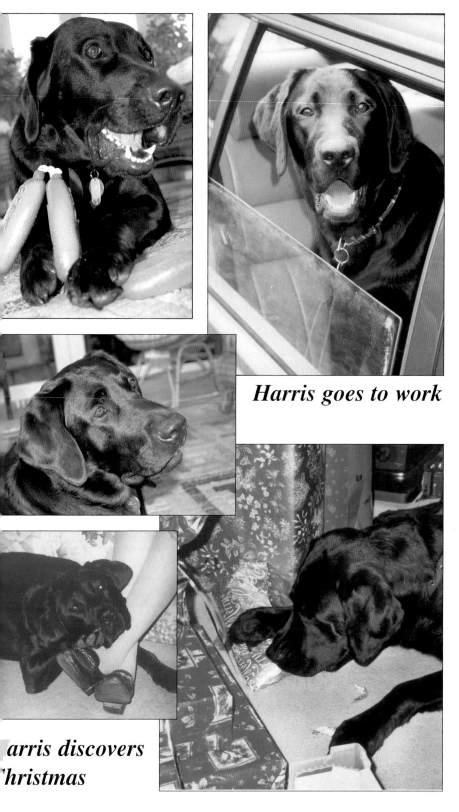

Harris goes to work

*Harris discovers
Christmas*

Harris on the Isle of Harris

liked, even down to the beach.

The moment the gate was open he was off. Before anyone could grab a lead or get to the gate before he did, he was away. To the left of the gate was a flock of sheep grazing lazily on the hillside. Harris did not hesitate. Here was his opportunity to show those sheepdogs what he could do - and it was a masterful performance.

He soon had a group of the sheep, about the same size as those which had been separated out by the shepherd in the training session, running as fast as their legs would carry them ahead of the advancing black apparition that we call Harris.

We had all seen the episode begin, but we were helpless to do anything about. Three different people were shouting HAAAAAAAARRRRRRRIIIIIIISSSSS at the top of their voices. He has very sharp hearing, so there is no doubt that he heard what we were saying, but he seemed completely oblivious to the imploring screams of a growing group of Harris-chasers.

We had discovered at an early age that when Harris's nose switches on his ears switch off, and he seems to go deaf. We were now discovering that this condition of temporary deafness has other causes also, one of which is a good chase after a willing flock of a sheep.

The flock of sheep headed for the sea, moving faster than I had ever seen sheep move before. Harris was in hot pursuit and quickly reached the stragglers. But what would he do next? No doubt he was re-running in his

mind what the shepherd had done the night before. An
exercise he had been carefully watching was separating
out one particular sheep from the flock so that the
shepherd could tend that sheep and that one alone.

Harris had no aggressive intent whatsoever towards
the sheep. He could easily have jumped on one or tried
to pull it to the ground, but he had no interest whatsoever
in doing any harm to the sheep or having a one-to-one
fight with these exciting white dogs, it was just the chase
that he loved.

The chasing group of humans were getting quickly out
of breath. Ahead Harris had isolated a group of about
twelve sheep, but there was one which was a bit separate
from the rest. Ah, Harris must have thought. Here's my
chance to show them that I can separate out a sheep from
the flock, just like those sheepdogs do.

He suddenly lost interest in the flock, much to their
relief, and turned all his attention on the single sheep
that was a bit away from the rest. Harris was now intent
on turning this particular sheep into a 400 metre hurdler.
Away the sheep went, jumping off the headland onto the
sand below, quickly followed by a leaping Harris who
was having such fun. Down on the beach Harris ran
round and round the sheep until the traumatised animal
could do nothing but collapse in an exhausted heap on
the sand and play dead.

This was not what Harris wanted, he still had lots of
running in him. What was wrong with this white dog,

hadn't his mother taught him how to play? When we finally caught up with them we were confronted with one white dog lying flat on its tummy, totally exhausted, and head to head with one black dog who was whining with disappointment that the white one had given up the game so prematurely.

The sheep was so motionless that we feared it had died of shock and was now dead on the beach. I was beginning to add up how much we would owe the shepherd for the dead sheep, and what we could give him by way of compensation for the unnecessary exercise Harris had given the rest of the flock.

Harris was so attentive to the sheep he had successfully isolated from the flock, just as he had been watching the shepherd do the previous night, that he almost didn't notice me slipping the lead over his head. At that critical moment the sheep suddenly jumped up and was off like an express train just as fast as its legs could carry it back to the security of the rest of the flock!

Harris set off again in hot pursuit, but this time the choker lead tightened round his neck and the game was over. Harris was now in serious trouble. He will never understand why he was in such trouble for doing exactly what the sheepdogs had been doing the previous night. It seemed so unfair!

We were very careful to see that the gate was never left open again. The shepherd was very gracious when we apologised to him, muttering something about the sheep needing some exercise. If he had really seen how much exercise his sheep had been given in such a short period of time he may have thought differently.

We were beginning to discover that there is more than one temptation through which Harris could do much harm and possibly, also, put himself in danger. In order for him to be safe he had to stay within the boundaries which would keep him out of harm's way.

The fence around the Harris house is a bit like the ten commandments that God put into the Bible. God warned us of the dangers we would encounter if we chose to step outside the provisions of God's law.

Many of the people we seek to help in our work have done exactly what Harris did. They have looked at what was happening on the other side of God's fence of life and looked for their opportunity to escape. And as soon as they saw a gate that was open they were away. But as the years have gone by they have reaped a harvest that they had not intended.

In another part of the Bible Paul talks about a law that applies to the whole of the human race when he says that, "whatsoever a man (or woman) sows, that shall he also reap". It is so true. If we sow bad seed in our lives we will reap a bad crop. If we go outside the fences of God's provision we will, eventually, reap a consequential bad harvest in our lives.

The fence was actually Harris's security. God's laws are our security. Stay within the fence and we can have great freedom. But if we choose to jump the fence and do our own thing we will eventually find that the consequences chain us into a prison of our own making.

Apart from just enjoying time with the family, my primary recreational activity on Harris is fishing. The isolation of being in a rowing boat in the middle of a Scottish loch is wonderfully restorative after a year of hectic activity. It helps when I am successful in catching a salmon or some trout, but catching fish is not an essential part of the recreational process. Just being alone in the middle of God's wonderful creation is healing in itself.

The way a salmon can leave its hatching place in the river, go to sea for a time and feed intensively in the Atlantic Ocean for a couple of years, before coming back as a fully grown salmon to the exact same river in which it was hatched is one of God's annual and extraordinary miracles of nature.

So far Harris has not been with me in the boat when I have actually caught one of these wonderful fish. That is an adventure yet to come. But when I have brought fish home he has taken more than a passing interest in the catch. Whether it's the smell or the taste of fresh fish I don't know, but he is definitely very interested. So much so that it took us some considerable time to retrieve a sea-trout from his jaws, after he had pounced on one of the catch and given it an unexpected tour of the perimeter fence! He rarely takes his eyes off me when I am out in the boat. He sits and stares intently as I row out into the loch, just waiting for the moment when he can welcome me back to shore.

As Harris has always kept me in his view while I am fishing, in just the same way God keeps us in his view. He knows the way we go and what we do. When we make mistakes he longs for us to come back to Him and receive forgiveness. He rejoices when we walk in His ways and are able to enjoy His blessing on our lives.

It's only as we and Harris together have enjoyed all the different activities of life on the island that we realise how perfectly named he was, in spite of his escapades with the sheep. The name fits his character and he seems to love adventuring on the island just as much as we do.

At the end of the day he lies contentedly snoring, dreaming about the day's activities and, no doubt, planning what fun he is going to have the following day. Neither he nor us wanted to leave the island and come home. But there's always another day to look forward to and maybe next time Harris won't chase the sheep and he will be in the boat with me catching a salmon.

Chapter 12
Harris Goes to Work

Harris not only changed our personal routines at home, but we also had to consider what we would do when we both had to go to work. Do we leave him at home all day, or should we try taking him with us?

We had heard various horror stories from other labrador owners who would come home after a few hours and discover their home had been trashed by an energetic undisciplined dog. We are grateful that this has never been our experience, and he was always very well behaved when we left him at home, but we did feel sorry for him and thought that he would probably fret through loneliness if he was left too often and too long.

So we began to experiment with taking him to work - not that we would take him into the offices every day, that would be too much of a distraction if such visits were any more than an occasional adventure. First we just left him in the car for periods in a place where he could be seen from the office. No problem - he was perfectly behaved and we could go out from time to time and take him for a walk in the beautiful grounds. Some of the staff began to volunteer to take him walks as well and so before long he was getting more walks and attention at the office than he was getting at home.

The final stage of his office acclimatisation was to leave the car in the courtyard where most staff would pass through several times a day, with the rear door of the estate car left wide open and Harris, tied with his long lead to the rear of the car. He just loved it and has never been any problem just sitting there waiting for the next person to pass, most of whom would give him a pat or talk to him as they went by.

But then we began to appreciate that Harris was not only benefiting from being at work with us, but he was developing an important role in his own right! One of the courses that Fiona has developed over the years is called *God's Creativity in You*, or *Healing Through Creativity*. The course was not just a series of teaching sessions but consisted of short teaching times followed by the opportunity to do many creative things, ranging from painting or pottery to wood carving or card-making, and numerous other activities as well.

This particular course has attracted a lot of people, many of whom have never had the opportunity to enjoy themselves doing creative things. When I was away teaching overseas, and Fi was conducting this course at home, she would take Harris in to work each day and leave him in the back of the car. It was amazing to see how many people on the course could relate easily to Harris and would talk about their problems while stroking him or sharing in a walk around the grounds.

One of the activities on the Creativity Course is a guided walk around the gardens, through the woods and along the canal. The purpose of the walk is for the leader to spend time pointing out significant things about the trees, the wild flowers, the wild life and other aspects of God's wonderful creation. On one occasion I was entrusted with the guided walk in the absence of the usual leader, so I decided to take Harris along as well.

While we did look at many interesting things, ranging from the extraordinary soft bark of giant Wellingtonia trees to the micro-life which lay hidden beneath a rotting log, it was Harris that most people wanted to talk about. I finished up telling them some of the parables of Harris as we walked along the canal and found that the truth behind the parables was sinking in. People were being really helped. Harris was discovering his own personal role as a counsellor without ever needing to say a word!

We have often had to help people who, in their early years, had been starved of opportunities to both give and receive affection and love or had been betrayed and abused by those who should have protected them. When this happens it can leave people deeply scarred emotionally and they find that giving and receiving affection from a dog can be a very non-threatening way of beginning to express love in a safe way. So Harris began to take work in his stride and lapped up all the attention he was getting!

There is something special about being able to look into a labrador's eyes. Their responsive look can bring such comfort. It sometimes seems as though they understand everything you are saying, without you even needing to speak out your thoughts. The look of love in their eyes empathises with whatever it is you are going through.

In Harris's case, when he is patiently waiting by the car at the office, he is also adept at being able to use this communication skill to his own personal advantage! He can easily make anyone who passes by feel sorry for him and want to spend a few moments playing with him or stroking him, before continuing on their way past his parking place! His preferred way of helping anyone out of their 'blues' is to invite you to play any sort of game with him.

If there is the end of a tissue hanging from a pocket, it will be surreptitiously and gleefully extracted. He loves to give coat sleeves a gentle tug of welcome or pick up any nearby object and plonk it on your lap as much as to say "What do you think of that then?"

Harris's friendly outgoing nature is either a 'bother' to people who are not keen on dogs or a 'delight' to whose who are. His favourite way of bonding with people is to bring the remains of one of his bones to your feet or hold it invitingly in his mouth, nudging your knees with it and not giving up until you get hold of one end of it while he chews the other. While doing this his large labrador eyes would gaze adoringly up, appreciating the sheer joy of sharing companionship with you, doing something he really enjoys.

People may not come up to you and nudge you with their favourite bones, but in a very similar sort of way they do enjoy talking with you about their favourite subject. They will sometimes keep on 'nudging' you with their conversation until you put down what you are doing and devote a few exclusive minutes to them, talking about something that really matters to them personally.

We can all do this in different ways. Each of us has things we love to talk about. Sometimes, the person we are talking with may not really be wanting to spend time just then, being distracted from whatever else they are doing, but we keep on nudging them with our 'bone' until we know we've been heard! Somehow or other, when we have managed to obtain those few exclusive moments of conversation we feel noticed. We feel valued when someone else has given us some of their time and their attention.

Sharing companionship, whether this is expressed through shared laughter, shared conversation, shared sorrow or shared work is one of the ways God made us to enjoy both Him and each other. None of us were designed by Him to live in isolation. When we return to the car after a day at the office or come home after leaving him there for a while, we are always met by Harris's faithful welcome, constantly wagging tail and his evident delight at being with us again. We are encouraged and comforted by his unconditional love and acceptance. He never fails to tell us he loves us in his own inimitable way.

In the same way God delights to enjoy our company. His love for us is unconditional and He never fails to hear our heart when we turn to him. The essence of prayer is not just turning to God when we are desperate, although he will always hear a cry of desperation, but having an ongoing relationship and fellowship with him. Relationship with Harris is not something that we turn on and off and only get involved in when we are desperate, it is a constant and personal experience. In the same way, God desires our relationship with Him to be a constant and personal experience also.

Whatever it is we are doing Harris loves to be included. He doesn't just want us to participate in the things he likes doing as a dog, such as sniffing the hedgerows, but he also loves to share in our other activities as well and be part of who we are.

Sometimes people get the mistaken idea that God is only interested in us when we are involved in Church activities. Nothing could be father from the truth. While there is no doubt that times of fellowship with God in worship services are important to Him, He loves us for who we are, whether we are at work, at play or at church and delights when we include Him in all that we do.

Harris not only enjoys his days at the office, he welcomes them. He just loves to enjoy all those relationships. He loves to play with us, travel with us and be anywhere that we are, whatever it us we are doing. Every part of our lives seems to matter to him, just as every part of our lives matters to God, but in a deeper and much more profound way than we could ever dream possible.

When Fiona had that first inkling of an idea to buy me a labrador for my birthday, she had no concept then of what God had in store for us through that tiny bundle of adorable fur. In reality, it has not been without its pressures, frustrations and sheer hard work, but as we have persevered, almost every day something interesting has happened that has surprised and delighted us. Getting Harris was a simple step of faith, but there is no way now that we would want to turn the clock back!

At times living a Christian life is not easy either. There are often difficulties that have to be overcome as we press on with walking in God's ways in obedience to His Word. It takes a step of faith to start the journey, but for those who choose to follow Him, there are also great blessings and rewards as well.

We often teach people that God has a loving purpose for each one of us and that as we persevere in fellowship with Him, we will not only know the joy of being totally fulfilled, but that He will be constantly surprising us with what he does in our lives and with the enjoyment of serving Him with a glad and thankful heart.

Chapter 13
Harris Discovers Christmas

Harris had been with us just one month when his first Christmas day dawned. He was still only three months old and everyday was an extraordinary adventure for an ever-curious labrador pup. But this was to be his best and most adventuresome day ever!

Christmas in our home has always been a big family occasion, but we have never lost sight of what we are celebrating amidst all the activities of the season. It has always been a wonderful holiday opportunity for different members of the family, who may not see very much of each other in the months in between, to not only celebrate God's wonderful gift of His son, but also renew family relationships.

Harris's first Christmas season was to be one of those never to be forgotten Christmases when all the members of the family from afar, young and old alike, first got to know the latest addition to the family. Both our Mums, all our children and grandchildren, my brother and various friends would all be involved at some time or other over the holiday period.

Even as a very young pup Harris seemed to recognise that boisterous play was alright with some people but not with our elderly Mums. Fortunately both Mums love dogs and having the opportunity to see and enjoy Harris was a joy for them both, even though they were approaching ninety at the time! The fun of giving Harris titbits was fully appreciated by both Harris and our Mums and they were really going to enjoy watching Harris experiencing his first Christmas.

My Mum was very impressed with Harris's discernment when it came to biscuits. It was assumed that an enthusiastic pup would be quite happy to sit for any old biscuit that was on offer - but not Harris! Plain old rich tea biscuits were nothing to Harris when compared with the added flavour of digestive biscuits. Before gulping down the tit-bit he would give it a good sniff and if it was a rich tea biscuit he would withdraw his nose from the offending object and wait until Mum changed the morsel to a piece of digestive, which he gratefully swallowed with obvious appreciation!

Fiona's Mum lives much closer than mine and is a more regular visitor. When she arrives Harris always takes an intense interest in her hand-bag. He quickly learnt that before leaving her home she would always hide a suitable treat there for him. Sometimes, especially when the treat was a sausage or something similar, the smell was so tantalising that nothing else could happen until Harris had devoured the contents of her hand-bag! Not only did the Mums love Harris, but he loved them!

Christmas was also going to be Harris's first opportunity to play with human puppies, when the grand-children came to stay, and to meet my older brother David, on what was to be his last family Christmas before he knew that cancer was beginning to take its toll on his body.

David was only going to be able to enjoy two more Christmases with us, before he lost the battle with this terrible disease. He had passed away before Harris was even three years old. But in those precious few days before he died, when we were all saying our good-byes to David, he said to each of us how much he loved us and then, turning to me, he said "And I love Harris too!" David had specially enjoyed Harris's company on his annual Christmas visit. Harris has the capacity of making everyone welcome and in some way or other wheedling his way into their heart!

The arrival of the grand-children was very exciting for Harris! Being much about his size, and full of the same sort of instant energy, they were wonderful play-mates. But as with our two Mums, Harris seemed to know just how far he could go in playing with them. It would have been so easy with his sharp teeth and bonding body to have unintentionally hurt them as they romped around, but nothing untoward ever happened and Harris has proven himself to be adept at entertaining both the very old and the very young, as well as everyone in between!

All families have different Christmas traditions. We have always opened our presents early on Christmas morning, then gone to church and had a very late lunch. Harris loves both parcels and turkey! So I am sure he thinks that the whole idea of Christmas Day celebrations and feasting was specially invented to entertain him.

The turkey gets put in the oven somewhere about 7.00am and gently roasts away throughout the morning. But even though the oven is supposed to be air tight, it's not very long before the smell of roasting turkey fills the whole house. Everyone's salivary glands are working overtime from an early hour!

For Harris this was both heaven and sheer torture at the same time. Heaven because the smell of roasting turkey or chicken has proven to be his most tantalising nasal experience of them all and torture because he can smell it for hours before he has the opportunity of stopping the salivary glands from working, through actually eating some turkey for himself!

The cards and decorated tree had been put up some time before Christmas. Some of the parcels under the tree had already proved too much for a curious labrador and had to be re-wrapped before they could be handed out on Christmas morning.

His biggest pre-Christmas problem were the presents labelled for Harris that contained special doggy treats and from which emanated exciting smells! And then there were the chocolate tree decorations. Well, by the time Christmas came all those hanging from the lower branches had disappeared. But no-one seemed to mind. The only certain thing was that Harris knew where they'd gone! It was all part of the fun.

And then came Christmas morning. Harris was in close attendance when the turkey was being prepared for the oven, but with so many other things happening at the same time he just didn't know what to do - he wanted to be everywhere at once.

When it came to opening the parcels there was only one place he wanted to be, right in the centre of the action. Many times we had had to restrain him from tearing some packet or other apart with his teeth, but now he must have been very confused. For here were these strange humans who, on every other day of the year would tell him not to do something, that now they were all doing themselves! He didn't let such scruples interfere with the sheer unadulterated pleasure he was getting from helping everyone open their parcels! And then tearing round and round the room with the torn pieces of paper as a prize. He couldn't understand, though, why we didn't chase after him to get the prize out of his mouth.

And then, joy of joys, he was not only allowed to help everyone else with their presents he was given a carefully wrapped present of his own. Several layers of paper, designed to give him a game along the way, were torn off in seconds, and there, right at the heart of the parcel was a large cloth duck - looking exactly like the real thing. Because he was still so small, and the duck was so huge, the sight of him parading round the room, carrying this retrieved duck so proudly in his mouth, reduced everyone to tears of laughter.

Nearly three years later he still walks round with the same duck in his mouth. Even though he could have torn duck to shreds in seconds, if he had wanted, amazingly he has never once set about dismembering the creature. Labradors have incredibly soft mouths when it comes to carrying game. They rarely inflict any damage on the bird. All Harris's game retrieving instincts have always prevailed when it comes to duck. In spite of heavy use, duck still looks good for a few more seasons of retrieving! The same is true of other soft toys he has been given from time to time.

The present giving session was a huge success. Everyone was pleased with the presents they had received and there was now a massive amount of paper which stood like a mountain in the middle of the room, with Harris sitting on top of it with his duck in his mouth. "Why can't every day be like this?" he seemed to be saying.

He had received various other Christmas treats in his parcels, including edible ones which he quickly devoured. Filled with tasty snacks, he then rested while we were all at Church, preparing himself for the next, and most exciting, part of the proceedings, Christmas Dinner!

With so many extra bodies seated around our farm-house kitchen table, every available space was filled to capacity with everything from cutlery to drinks and, of course, the special Christmas table napkins. These were Harris's signal for Christmas fun.

As soon as we were all seated, and even while we were saying grace, Harris slipped under the table and took his place in the middle of the floor. Of course, any food that accidentally fell to the floor was fair game. It would be gone almost before it hit the floor. But his favourite occupation was to prowl under the table and watch for any person who was not hanging on to their Christmas table napkin!

With a deft movement of his head, he placed his jaws in exactly the right position to gently grip the edge of the napkin and then, with a swift almost imperceptible tug, the napkin was his. Oliver Twist could not have picked the pockets of his unsuspecting victims on the streets of London any more effectively than Harris removed the napkins from people's laps.

He would then quietly shred the napkin on the floor before continuing his thieving exploits around the table. One by one he managed to capture most of the napkins at various stages of the meal.

The starters were rather boring for Harris. Melon and prawns or a Christmas soup were not for him. He was waiting for the real food to start coming his way, by which I mean turkey. As soon as the turkey was out of the oven and standing on the serving table waiting to be carved, Harris was there in attendance. He sat there like a smartly dressed, velvet coated flunkie ready to do anything to please his master, provided a suitable tip was pressed into his paw at regular intervals.

In reality, it's very hard to carve a large turkey without numerous little bits falling off the sides of the carving dish. And what would one do with them if there wasn't such a worthy cause sitting drooling at one's feet? Harris learnt that if he made a real nuisance of himself he would get told off and would get nothing, so instead of whining or barking he would sit patiently, looking straight up at the source of all those juicy aromas and every now and again shuffle his bottom on the floor, just to let you know he was still there.

In between the shuffles there would be the almost imperceptible, but nevertheless discernible, little whimpers together with a gathering stream of saliva, to continually remind me that I was not only carving the turkey for the whole of the family, but making provision for man's best friend.

Usually when Fi wasn't looking a piece of juicy turkey would get slipped into a waiting mouth. All his food was invariably placed in his bowl for him to eat from there, but this was Christmas and who would really want to deny Harris the opportunity of sharing in the feast at the same time as everyone else?

Once everything was dished up and everyone's plate was piled high with turkey, roast potatoes, parsnips, brussel sprouts, cauliflower and cranberry sauce, Harris resumed his former place of guard duty beneath the kitchen table. After all, wasn't it his job to ensure that no stray food could ever land on the kitchen floor?

A further supply of Christmas napkins had been handed out, together with an even more extraordinary part of the festivities as far as Harris was concerned - the Christmas crackers. What were these things that were torn apart with a bang, sometimes scattering their contents all over the floor, and finally providing all these mad humans with a hat such as Harris had never seen before?

The bangs didn't worry him - somewhere in his stored, instinctive memory was probably a bit of information that told him this was training for the gun - but those hats, they were something different! He could not understand what they were for. His quizzical expression seemed to be saying, "If only people knew how silly they all looked". But the hats did give him something more to pounce on, and tear to shreds, as one by one they fell off heads that were not made to measure for these one-sized Christmas headgear!

The smell of Christmas pudding had the effect of slowing down some of the appetites around the table, as people remembered that they needed to leave some space for the final round of Christmas fare. Harris benefited enormously from this situation as one by one people came to the edge of their food intake limits and small piles of food were left at the edge of people's plates.

As the plates were cleared, every single bit of Christmas turkey skin and meat, together with a healthy surplus of vegetables got tipped into his bowl. While the pudding was being dished up I fussed around the turkey remains, rescuing many delectable bits for my waiting friend. Sharing food is a very bonding experience for humans. I was discovering that it was an equally bonding experience between one man and his dog!

Small helpings of puddings were, for some courageous souls, followed by second helpings, and when the feasting was all over, everyone declared once again that Fi's dinner, this year, had excelled all others and was the best they had ever tasted!

After his first Christmas dinner, Harris could have said that with absolute truthfulness, his tail adequately expressing his appreciation as he waddled through to the lounge and joined the rest of the family in what turned out to be a corporate snooze. Dogs, like humans, can also enjoy an after-lunch sleep!

Later in the afternoon Harris's need for a walk gave

my brother and I a much enjoyed and remembered time of personal sharing as we accompanied Harris for a walk along the canal.

In most families, Christmas time is also an opportunity for playing games, but Harris wasn't very keen on the sort of participatory games which he couldn't join in. And he definitely couldn't understand why we weren't pleased when he walked across the playing area of a board game, scattering the pieces everywhere to loud screams of Haaaarrrriiissssss!

He didn't like either the occasional noisy hilarity that didn't involve an adventure with him. His way of coping with it all was to hide behind the furniture until it was all over, much like people must have hidden in air-raid shelters during the war, waiting for the all clear!

Harris's first Christmas was totally memorable, as has each succeeding Christmas when the whole process is repeated year after year. This year, however, it will be different without David, but I will always have that memory of David smiling at me from his hospital bed and saying, "I love Harris too!"

For as long as I can remember Christmas memories have been powerful reminders of important family times. Times which have been precious and strategic in one's personal history. When I was young my parents had little surplus money at any time of the year, but they always managed to make Christmas a very special family time, and sacrificed themselves personally so that they could give my brother and I at least one special present each year, some of which even now, two generations later, are unforgettable and important! We always knew what Christmas was all about and why we gave presents to each other.

Yes, many of the things we do at Christmas may seem a long way removed from the simplicity of the stable in Bethlehem where Jesus was born. And the increasing secularisation of the Christmas season may have meant that very few Christmas cards these days make any mention of the reason for the season. Yet, for those with eyes that are open to see and hearts that are willing to understand the Christ of Christmas will still make His joyous presence felt in the lives of those who are still willing to receive Him.

Harris will never understand why we celebrate Christmas, but the fun we all had sharing together as a family will never be forgotten. I believe it gladdens the heart of God when he sees his children enjoying themselves together. But I know it gladdens his heart far more when those who are celebrating the birthday of his Son do so with glad and thankful hearts.

Postscript

By now you will have realised that Harris is not a perfect dog! But that he does have many wonderful redeeming characteristics - and we love him! Labradors are such enthusiastic dogs, that love for labradors really does have to cover a multitude of sins!

Our lives changed radically when Harris first arrived, but even though we have had our share of frustrations at his behaviour, and even times of anger when he has really messed up, we have never once wished we hadn't got him.

He may have made us want to tear our hair out on occasions, especially when he was stretching the tolerance levels of our friends and visitors, but when he sits on the kitchen floor, with his head on one side, as if he is saying "sorry", forgiveness isn't hard.

Harris's natural naughtiness and occasional rebellion against his owners is a very close parallel to sin against God in human beings. It may have tested our love to the limits, but even though the limits have sometimes been far beyond where we would like them to have been, they have never gone beyond the limits of our love.

Having Harris has taught us so much about the relationship God desires to have with mankind. And just as we have never reached the limits of love for our black labrador, God has never been pushed beyond the limits of his love for the human race.

One of the most well-known verses in the Bible says that God loved the world so much (even in its rebellious sinfulness) that He sent His Son to die for the sins of mankind, so that anyone could come back to God, ask for forgiveness, accept Jesus as his Saviour and receive new life (John 3:16). No-one is beyond the limits of God's love. He is always there when we turn again to Him.

Even when Harris had totally let us down by chasing the sheep in Harris, or chewing the precious pocket computer of one very special friend or redesigning the much loved leather shoes of another, we still loved him. Every one of these incidents was a further opportunity to teach and train him about what's right and what's wrong. Slowly he learned the lessons and as we were patient with him, he gradually responded to the love and the discipline we were giving him.

Harris is now three years old. He's just beginning to show signs of settling down to a slightly more mature lifestyle. But I hope he never loses the spunk that has made him such an enjoyable and adventuresome member of the family. And we will always be on the lookout for more parables, as we seek to learn fresh lessons God has for us through the experience of living with our inimitable four legged friend!

If Harris could write his own story he would no doubt write that he now has perfectly trained owners! He is able to extract a tit-bit, treat or game whenever his owners or family are around. He believes the newly built conservatory is his new kennel provided so that he can survey all his territory and make rapid exits to chase squirrels, cats or the rabbit population whenever he desires.

The car is also his own personal mobile home from which many adventures ensue. Roast dinners are cooked especially for him and he awaits his portion with anticipation dribbling from his mouth. His annual holiday is the equivalent of a world cruise where he pursues his favourite interests of swimming, beach-combing, rock-climbing and romping in the heather.

The length of his walks he determines by the degree of sniffs and smells he wants to indulge in along the way.

His anchors go down and his owners are rendered powerless until he is ready to continue! Every visitor to the house is given a larger than life welcome and he believes them to have come simply to be his playmate.

Perhaps the final parable of Harris should be that our experiences with him speak more about us as owners than about him, the dog! It is very freeing for us as humans to know that we do not have to be perfect to be loved!

About the Authors

Peter and Fiona Horrobin are Directors of The Christian Trust, the UK Registered Charity which is responsible for the work of Ellel Ministries International. They travel extensively, teaching and training people on how to bring hope through Christian healing.

Both Peter and Fiona have always been concerned to teach in such a way that people easily remember the lessons. Shortly after Harris became a member of the family, they began to share some of their experiences in raising a labrador pup by way of illustration for some of their teaching. It was immediately obvious that people loved the stories and were remembering the lessons they illustrated.

When Peter returned home from a teaching conference in Germany with a present for Harris from a grateful conference organiser, Peter realised that Harris had come to stay as a member of the team! People began to ask for copies of the parables and so before long the vision for this book was born out of popular demand!

Both Peter and Fiona have many and varied interests, but the arrival of Harris has had a limiting effect on the amount of time available to pursue their other interests and hobbies. In years gone by Peter has written and edited a number of professional texts on subjects relating to Architecture and Building and was also responsible for editing and compiling The Complete Catalogue of British Cars. He is also one of the compilers of the widely popular hymn and song book, Mission Praise.

The Parables of Harris

*All enquiries relating to this book, including
information in respect of publishing rights in other
languages or territories and correspondence for the
authors, should be addressed to the publishers at:*

Lancaster Editorials Ltd.,
P.O.Box 761,
Preston,
PR3 0WX.

Printed in England by Clays Ltd., St. Ives Plc.

All photographs used in this book are also copyright
and were taken by the authors, Paul Stanier,
Johann Hanekom and Otto Bixler.